LUCK,
COURAGE,
& MIRACLES

LUCK, COURAGE, & MIRACLES

Surviving the Jewish Ghettos of Poland and Escaping the Nazi Death Camps

SIGMUND WEISS

Archway Publishing books may be ordered through booksellers or by contacting:

Archway Publishing
1663 Liberty Drive
Bloomington, IN 47403
www.archwaypublishing.com
844-669-3957

Because of the dynamic nature of the Internet, any web addresses or links contained in this book may have changed since publication and may no longer be valid. The views expressed in this work are solely those of the author and do not necessarily reflect the views of the publisher, and the publisher hereby disclaims any responsibility for them.

Any people depicted in stock imagery provided by Getty Images are models, and such images are being used for illustrative purposes only.
Certain stock imagery © Getty Images.

A blank map of World War II Europe from www.historicalmapchart.net served as template for the illustration of Sigmund Weiss' journeys.

ISBN: 978-1-6657-3260-4 (sc)
ISBN: 978-1-6657-3259-8 (hc)
ISBN: 978-1-6657-3261-1 (e)

Library of Congress Control Number: 2022919884

Printed in the United States of America.

Archway Publishing rev. date: 08/09/2023

This book is dedicated to Sigmund Weiss's grandchildren, Michael, David, and Jonny. As children and young adults, they learned of his experiences firsthand, thus becoming "third-generation survivors." To those who deny that the Holocaust ever happened, they will be able to carry on telling the story and truth as witnesses of its devastating effect on their grandfather. Hopefully, they will pass this book down to the next generation: Maggie, Peter, Iris, Genevieve, Hazel, and Albert. My father's great-grandchildren will verify the authenticity of the Holocaust from his stories and videos retelling his third-generation grandsons about the hardships, killings, and tragedies of World War II. Remembrance of the Holocaust is more important now than ever, as Russia's unprovoked attack on Ukraine has raised the terrifying specter of a third world war.

I also dedicate this book to a dear friend, Maitland DeLand, MD, without whom this book would not have happened. My father's history would have remained incomplete, hidden in a 1998 German-language booklet published by the White Rose Society in partnership with the Deutsch-Israelische Gesellschaft. After learning of this condensed version, Dr. DeLand insisted that it be completed. She funded several months of professional interviews with my father over Skype. After enlisting editing assistance from her son Andrew, who is also very interested in the history and atrocities of WWII, she sent the transcript of the interviews to a professional editor. I extend my heartfelt thanks to them.

The final dedication is to my wife, Margaret Weiss, who was such a superb mother to our three sons and a substitute daughter to my father Sigmund. Her assistance was invaluable in his final years, allowing him to live out his life as he wished in the same Rego Park apartment where I grew up, below the landing pattern of jets flying into New York's LaGuardia Airport. I also want to thank Judy Steven and Sergio Rivera, whose wonderful care helped my father to live until the age of ninety-six. Not even COVID-19 could kill "Sigi" in March of 2020. He died peacefully in his sleep on the evening of January 31, 2022, my sixty-ninth birthday.

Robert A. Weiss, M.D.

CONTENTS

PREFACE

When people ask me why I wanted to tell my story, I tell them that it is to do my part to preserve what happened, both to me as an individual and to the millions of other Jews, many of whom were less fortunate than I and did not emerge from those deeply troubled years with their lives. Every year, there are fewer and fewer people who can recall these terrible events, and it is important for those of us with firsthand knowledge to testify. In our present life during the COVID worldwide pandemic, recalling this history of human cruelty becomes even more compelling. Humankind too often seems discontented with just appreciating what one has and must satisfy cravings for disruption. But maybe after COVID-19, this will change.

And so here is the story of my family and me, Sigmund Weiss; and while this story is specific to me, it is not so unique that it doesn't apply to all humans persecuted, hunted, and slaughtered through the twentieth century. Recalling and documenting—this is how we never will forget. And we must not forget the fact that six million Jews were murdered in a program that was government initiated, enabled, and condoned that we refer to as "the Holocaust." While two-thirds of all Jews living in Europe at the time were killed, Hitler's real purpose was genocide: to erase the Jewish people from the earth. Like the way that a virus wants to infect every living person on the earth. Hitler failed in his plan, but in the process crushed so many dreams, uprooted and smashed family trees, and changed the life passage of survivors and subsequent generations forever. Since those who perished cannot tell their stories, I have preserved the story of one unlikely survivor, myself, which I attribute to a combination of luck and miracles, but most humbly the courage to keep on living.

Sigmund Weiss

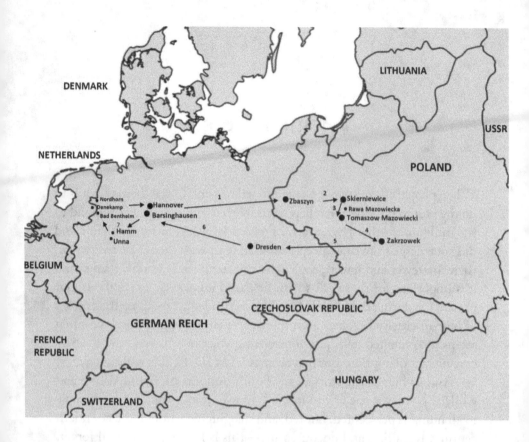

The Journeys of Sigmund Weiss 1938–1945

1	1938
2	1939–1941
3	1941
4	1941–1942
5	1942
6	1942–1945
7	1945

Map of Sigmund's Journeys 1938–1945

Sigmund Weiss

FOREWORD

Growing up as the only child of Sigmund and Renee Weiss, I remember that during workdays, the atmosphere at home was peaceful. My mother stayed home; she vacuumed daily, even when the vacuum hose had become so worn that I suspect most of the dust came right back out from the cracks. I walked to school and came home to do homework. My father would come home complaining about the traffic from Manhattan as he preferred driving instead of the bus or subway. He almost always had to stop and buy food like a rotisserie chicken before parking in the garage under Park City Estates. The name did not fit the complex of sixteen-story brick buildings that faced the Long Island Expressway as they were neither a park nor an estate. Maybe the name "park" referred to the large area of parking under the five-building complex where he walked daily through the large sooty exhaust-filled garage carrying our dinner and groceries as my mother did not like to leave the safety of the apartment. My mother had been refused entry from Austria to the US then refused in Cuba and finally admitted to El Salvador, so she was reluctant to travel anywhere again.

While weekdays were orderly, weekends often began with discord. My father wanted to go out and not be trapped in the relatively small apartment; my mother wanted to stay home. About every few weeks, my father would take out a tin box from the top dresser drawer to show me photographs. As he would show me pictures of his father and sister, he would often shed tears as he replayed in his mind the scenes that you will experience reading this autobiography. The cruelness of the Nazi regime was very much burned into my memory as if it was happening at that very moment to me as well. Dates, cities, ghettos, time of escape, arrests, close encounters with death, and bicycling toward Holland were often repeated; but for some reason, I could not ever remember the exact sequence. This is common for second-generation Holocaust survivors.

To change the subject and improve his mood on the weekends, my father and I would go on outings to the Bronx botanical garden or Bronx Zoo where the visions of the violence, beatings, shootings, and feelings of being trapped would soon be contained until the next weekend. My mother would always stay home. The beauty of the botanical gardens would temporarily replace the memories of Hitler's reign. In 1970, my father bought a used twenty-eight-foot fiberglass boat, which he named *Amazon* so that we would have a regular weekend retreat away from the memories, away from the photos in the tin box, and away from the daily vacuuming in the apartment.

When I enrolled at Columbia University and took a writing course as part of the freshman curriculum, I realized how important it was to record all the horrible events that he had gone through in as much detail as possible for additional documentation of the Holocaust. I encouraged him to write his story, but often he would break down into a deep sadness reliving the moments of horror as he was scribbling them down on a yellow notepad, but he was able to finish a shorter version in German. He would not be able to sleep if he was writing after dinner, which usually wasn't until 7:00 PM. With the help of a doctor colleague of mine, we encouraged him to dictate his experiences over Skype to a former *NY Times* author who wrote them down exactly as his spoken word. That is how the first version of this English language book came to be. The first version was written in German, left out many details, but was thankfully published by the White Rose Society in October 1988. Sigmund was honored for it at a ceremony in Hanover, Germany, hosted by the mayor and covered by German media.

I accompanied him on that trip and went to high school-sponsored events where students could ask him about his experiences. One student asked, "If you were treated so badly, why didn't you leave Germany then?" My father became angry, answered abruptly, and we exited the high school in Hanover. When you read this book, you will clearly understand why.

Robert Weiss, M.D.

CHAPTER ONE

THERE'S NO PLACE LIKE HOME—
LIFE BEFORE HITLER

W hat do you think of when you remember your hometown? Perhaps you still live there; remembering is easy although with the passage of time, it may have changed around you, for better or worse. If you moved away as a young adult seeking new adventures, perhaps your hometown is a place you remember fondly, somewhere you still feel connected to, somewhere full of echoes of a carefree youth. The schoolhouse, the park, the church, the factory, the movie theater, the library—around every corner is a place that has an association with family and friends and belonging.

Now imagine your beloved hometown as somewhere you left not of your own free will but because you were forced to leave. You did not do anything to deserve exile; rather, almost overnight, friends and enemies alike decided you didn't belong. Now the schoolhouse, the park, the house of worship, the factory, the movie theater, and the library are dark places that signify danger, places where death might be lurking.

For me, this nightmare version of a hometown was Barsinghausen, Germany, where I was born on August 12, 1925.

The last stop on the Line 10 commuter railway from Hanover, Barsinghausen, is now a large town of more than thirty thousand people; but back when I was young, the population was maybe half that. Historically, Barsinghausen was predominately a mining town. If the townspeople didn't work in the coal mines or fields, they worked in the shops that catered to the farmers and miners. My maternal grandfather worked in the mines and my father too (as a prisoner of war). By the time I was born, however, the mines were shut. The veins of coal had been depleted, and mining there had become unprofitable. The mines were boarded up, but sometimes we kids would go and play among the remnants of the industrial past in a natural landscape forever scarred by humankind.

Following the closing of the mines, the Barsinghausen economy had to diversify. Many of the inhabitants remained farmers, but the shopkeeping in town flourished. My father kept a shop, in which he worked as a tailor.

Even living in a smaller town, we did see tourists from the cities. Residents of Hanover often came to our town on day trips or for the weekend to enjoy the hotel spas, swimming pools, and baths in the town or to walk in the Deister, a chain of rolling hills in Lower Saxony (pictured in figure 1). There are old castles and funeral mounds from centuries ago littered across the Deister hills, and the area includes a large nature reserve, a stretch of protected woods five miles wide and twenty-five miles long, perfect for strolling. All this natural beauty made Barsinghausen something of a health resort then, as it still is today. The city people came to walk and cycle. They came for the fresh air and quiet.

Figure 1

While the city people came for weekend strolls down the trails in the woods, we, as locals, were free to enjoy the woods whenever we wanted. It was nice for us as children to live so close to such a place, and I am happy that before the troubles came, I was able to live there.

The hills are not so high—they top out at about four hundred meters—and it only takes an hour to reach the highest point. My father would take us up to the highest summit on Sunday walks. When I got a little older, I started going up with friends and other neighborhood kids; I enjoyed these sojourns very much. Eventually, though, once the Nazis took power, other kids stopped going with us because we were Jewish, and the sight of the hills became just one of the many sources of melancholy.

My Father

My father's name was Adolf Weiss. In those days, Adolf was a very common name in Germany, even among Jews, and not yet stigmatized by Hitler—the only Adolf many in the West know now.

My father was born in 1891 to a Polish Jewish family from Tomaszów Mazowiecki, Piotrków Province, which is not far from Lódz, though Tomaszów (pronounced "Toma-shuf") belonged to Russia at the time. (Much later, in 1939, his family's hometown became home to a ghetto of sixteen thousand five hundred imprisoned Jews, of which fifteen thousand were ultimately sent to concentration camps.)

Father had four sisters and one brother. His father, my grandfather, was a poor textile dyer in Tomaszów. As the oldest son, my father had to help support the family financially from an early age, which molded him into a strong man with much character. To help make money for his family, my father began learning how to work as a tailor at the tender age of eleven. By fourteen, he had begun making a living at it.

When he was only seventeen, my father was unexpectedly drafted into the czar's army. Like all draftees, he had to report for a medical to ensure he was fit to be a soldier. My father tried to avoid the draft. He declared his birth date as 1898, which would have made him about ten years old when he was drafted; but being slight and small for his age, he could pass for a child. Nevertheless, because he was healthy and strong, the army accepted him. He passed his medical, to his own chagrin, and was drafted.

My father was then sent for military training at Samarkand, which is near the border with Afghanistan, where he served three and a half years in the czar's army. He was then allowed to return home. His civilian life was to be short-lived, however. Within six months of returning home, he was redrafted. It was 1914, and the Great War had broken out. The czar needed trained soldiers like my father to fight for Russia (fig. 2).

Figure 2

Russian troops began pouring into East Prussia, my father among them, to fight against German troops under the command of General Hindenburg, a man who would later go on to be the German president and the man who would go down in history as the person who appointed Hitler chancellor of Germany.

Sigmund Weiss

The war did not go well for my father. In 1915, my father's brigade, like many in the army, was surrounded by German troops. Many of those in his brigade were killed; and the surviving soldiers, my father included, were captured, and sent to Germany as prisoners of war.

In Germany, my father was shuffled between several prisoner of war camps, first in Celle and later in Barsinghausen. The Barsinghausen camp was in the region of the coal mines, which were of strategic importance during World War I. My father was put to work in the mines, where my maternal grandfather worked as a civilian. They did not know each other at the time.

My father thrived within the camp as best as anyone could. He spoke Polish, Russian, and Yiddish—which has been the native language of all Jews in Eastern Europe since the thirteenth century. (Yiddish was derived from a combination of German and ancient Hebrew. Yiddish is about 90 percent German and only 10 percent Hebrew, but it is strongly associated with Jews nonetheless.)

His knowledge of languages allowed my father to become an interpreter at the POW camp in Barsinghausen. He also tailored uniforms and clothing for the patrol officers and their families. In exchange for these skilled services, my father gained the trust of his German captors and so enjoyed special privileges and freedoms.

By the end of his time at the Barsinghausen camp, my father was even allowed to wear civilian clothing and sometimes go out dancing. In those days, they had outdoor cafés, and while appearing to be little more than old farmhouses from the outside, they were big enough on the inside to host social occasions and were adapted for various purposes. They served as community centers where townspeople could go to talks, see movies, and attend dances and socials.

When I think of it now, it is strange that he would stay in the town where he had been a prisoner, but I guess his reason for staying was that he fell in love. Sometime during his imprisonment, my father met my mother, Lina Baeir, at a dance that took place at the Deister Hotel.

I realize now what an especially hard life my father had; his life was never truly his own. He had to work from a very young age to support his family, and then he was drafted twice and imprisoned. He was his own man for a period of only twenty years—from 1919 to 1939—but even during this time, his dream of freedom in America was curtailed by the needs of his new family. This dream was finally denied for the rest of his life by forced exile and ghetto incarceration. It is sad that he was never in his life truly free.

My Mother

My mother, Lina, was German—born and raised in Barsinghausen. She was the fourth of eight daughters, and her father worked in the very mines in which my father was held as a prisoner of war. Though the circumstances that brought my father there were less than ideal, I suppose he probably considered it serendipitous to have been taken there.

In 1919, the war ended, and my father was released from the camp. He and my mother were planning to marry, and my mother became pregnant with my sister (fig. 3A).

Figure 3A

However, their wedding plans presented a problem: my mother was raised as an Evangelical Lutheran, and my father was Jewish. In the 1920s, there was no kind of stigma to marrying a Jew, and my mother's family accepted my father into the family warmly. Unfortunately, it was an issue for my father, who took his faith and culture seriously. My mother was a gentile, and traditional Judaism frowned upon interfaith marriages. After discussing the matter with friends and family and, most importantly, my father's rabbi, they decided she would convert to Judaism.

While my father did want to maintain a Jewish household, we were not strictly Jewish. We observed the Sabbath—all the Jews in town did—but not every Saturday. We attended synagogue regularly but not rigidly. We went to a small synagogue in the hills that served the town's Jewish minority. The building was more of a converted stable really, but it was a worthy place of worship. There was a regular rabbi there and a regular teacher, both very nice. We had no problem attending these services in the beginning, but once the troubles began, it became sensible not to attend.

The synagogue kept us connected to the local Jewish community. We also bought our meat from a Jewish butcher because he stocked kosher meat, and we would often go to Hanover where we could get dried fish and matzo from Jewish vendors. Jews were a minority in Germany, but anti-Semitism was not so common before Hitler came to power.

Prior to getting married, my father had been planning to immigrate to America, where two of his sisters had gone after leaving Poland, but now he abandoned this plan. After so much time at war and then in the camps, he had saved only a few marks. And now he had a growing family to support. Rather than buy tickets to America, he stayed put in Barsinghausen and spent his last few marks on a new sewing machine to build a new life in Germany, in Barsinghausen, as a tailor.

I must confess that I often wonder how things might have been different had they gone to America rather than stayed in Europe. Germany proved not to be the best place for a Jewish family to make their home, but of course, they did not know this at the time as at first they were quite happy in Barsinghausen. They settled down, started a tailoring business, and raised their daughter, my sister Rosa who was born in 1919. I was born six years after Rosa. By the time I came along, Rosa was already known in town and even in neighboring villages as "beautiful little Rosa," the daughter of a Jewish tailor.

My Home

At first, my parents lived with my mother's family in their house. My parents both worked long, hard hours; but they were happy and soon had enough to buy their own house on the same street, Langenkampstrasse 15A, an old timber-frame house (fig. 3B). We moved there in 1928 when I was only three.

Figure 3B

I was too young to remember living with my grandpa Baier in his house, so my earliest childhood memories are of my parents' house. My father gutted and rehabbed the whole building. It was probably a modest house by some standards, but it was a good place to raise young children and a good place to be a child.

We were not rich, but I was too young to realize that money was tight. In truth, I felt like a little prince. I had everything a boy could possibly want in the world: I had hardworking parents who loved my sweet, beautiful sister and me; my best friend, Walter Plinke, lived on the same street as I did; and I owned a tricycle and a wooden horse. We had goats in the barn and chickens in the garden, where my father planted trees and I was allowed to plant my own flowers (fig. 3C). I liked the feel of putting my fingers into the soft dirt.

Figure 3C

What more could a child want? It was a good place to be a child, but then I was not aware there was so much evil in the world.

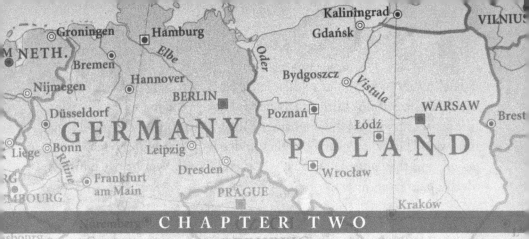

CHAPTER TWO

SHARP STONES IN MY SKIN— NAZISM COMES TO BARSINGHAUSEN

A s a child, I was as unaware of the political drama unfolding in Europe as I was of my parents' true financial situation. The fallout from the First World War was already setting the stage for World War II. The harsh terms of the Treaty of Versailles had many Germans feeling angry and resentful as if the treaties added insult to injury, and Hitler used this discontentment to start pounding the war drum. Nationalism was on the rise, and soon the specter of fascism would rear its ugly head.

But I knew none of this. I was too young to understand the hushed voices of adult conversations, too young to appreciate the context or the content. All I knew was that things were not good now in Germany and Europe, but times had been worse before. I knew that my father had known worse—he was a still-young man who had been drafted into half a decade of military service and spent the better part of the other half in a POW camp. My father told me that after the First World War, life was very bad, but things then got better and more prosperous, at least for them. As a tailor, he made a decent living making pants for the department stores, which brought in enough money to make ends meet comfortably. We were not rich, but we wanted nothing. Obviously, he had known worse times—but he now had a loving wife, a pretty daughter, and a son who looked up to him.

Life had its challenges, but in the 1920s, it was not so bad to be a Jew in Germany, not at all like later. My father believed everything would be okay if this Hitler character did not ascend to power. This was the consensus around Barsinghausen. The townspeople understood that this would be bad for everyone. They understood that Hitler wanted war again, and they understood that war is bad for all. War brings famine, death, pain, and misery.

Loss of Innocence

Ignorance can be bliss, but children do not stay naïve forever. The older I got, the more I took in. To this day, I still clearly remember the elections of 1932, the year I started school (fig. 4A.B). Over the radio and on flyers in town, you were exposed to propaganda pushing people to vote for the Social Democratic Party. *Vote for SPD! Vote for NSDAP! Vote for Hindenburg!*

Figure 4A.B

Hindenburg was growing old by this point, but he was widely viewed as the only presidential candidate who could beat Hitler in an election. He was a war hero—having served valiantly in both the Prussian Army and, later, in the German Army during the Great War. The people rejoiced when he was reelected.

All was in vain though. The political situation in Germany continued to deteriorate; and the Weimar Republic, which had been established by revolution after the war, was disintegrating. Despite his best attempts to resist Hitler's grasp on power, Hindenburg made Hitler chancellor in 1933, hoping that he and his cabinet could control Hitler. As we all know, it did not work out the way Hindenburg had, perhaps foolishly, hoped or imagined. When Hindenburg passed away the following year, Hitler declared the presidency "vacant" and declared himself, as chancellor, the head of the German state. There were no more elections. The office of the president would remain vacant. The Führer was the leader now.

Life, and especially school, became harder for me as a Jewish child. My friends—the same friends I had played with in the Diester hills and abandoned mines—stopped talking to me. Some of my friends told me their fathers had forbidden them to interact with me. That hurt. But it hurt more later when these same children, at first repentant, adopted the hateful attitudes and prejudices of their parents. They no longer needed to blame their parents for their bigotry. The cause of this was the Hitler Youth campaign.

Before Hitler began ascending to power, the other children and I got along swimmingly. The Christian kids would play with the Jewish kids. Everyone knew who was Protestant, who was Catholic, and who was Jewish, but no one cared. Their families didn't care. That was how it was for me in the first grade. But after the elections of 1932, everything changed.

Now my childhood friends began to abandon me, and other students began to bully me, picking fights that start with words and progressed to physicality.

My schoolmates became tyrants, each one a cruel little Hitler. They stopped verbally bullying me and now openly assaulted me, starting fights in the school's halls and in the playground. I fought back, which my parents did not like, but what else could I do? The little Hitlers marched up to me and yelled into my face and struck me wherever they could land a punch, so I had no choice but to hit back. Fight fire with fire. Give a black eye for a black eye. But there were many of them and only one of me, and so these fights sometimes ended in a beating. However, when they hit me, I learned how to hit back harder, and this made many of my tormentors afraid of me. Thankfully, I was strong for my age. This seemed to work at first, and my ability to fight kept their assaults at bay. But they got craftier in their bullying of me.

They began turning a teacher against me, a rather unjust and cruel man himself who was easy to provoke to anger. He would often punish students for no reason, but the other kids gave him plenty of reasons to punish me. He had a hard wooden cane that he liked to strike students with when they were bad. For me, I got the cane for the slightest infraction or often for nothing at all. The other students would start fights and get me to fight back then run and tell the teacher so that he would beat me with the cane.

The longer it went on, the worse it got. Gangs of schoolkids would follow me home and throw stones. When I turned around to face them, they scattered and ran away until I turned my back again. The stones stung when they hit my skin, but the worst part was the way they made me feel inside. I didn't understand their cruelty, and I certainly had not done anything to deserve it.

One day, a small sharp stone struck me in the head and lodged in my flesh. Blood trickled from the wound. When I got home and my father saw the blood, I thought he would be angry, but instead he was just concerned. This is when he realized my life would be in danger if I stayed at the secular school. I was pretty good at defending myself, but it was tiring: who wants to live that way? After three years at the school in Barsinghausen, I was transferred to a Jewish school in Hanover. I enjoyed this school and being around others in the same situation.

This segregated school became mandatory for all Jewish children once the Nazi Party began to take control of the country. My sister had attended only public schools, but I, six years younger, was now no longer allowed to. So from eleven to thirteen, I attended a Jewish school in Hanover as decreed by German law. Every morning, I would travel an hour by train to Hanover, like all the other Jewish children from the other villages surrounding Hanover. Despite the long commute, this school was much better for me. The school beatings stopped. Unfortunately, I still had to return home to Barsinghausen after school (fig. 5).

Figure 5

No Escape

The situation in Barsinghausen, and throughout Germany and Eastern Europe, continued to deteriorate throughout the rest of the 1930s. With Hitler as chancellor, anti-Semitic propaganda spread throughout the country. You heard it over the radio. You heard it everywhere. "Jews! Jews!" the people would scream contemptuously in the streets and over the airwaves. It was "Jews did this" and the "Jews did that." We were blamed for everything with Hitler both starting and fanning the flames of hatred between the German peoples.

As early as 1933, my parents were beginning to consider the future. They asked themselves, what now? The German state was passing laws against us, criminalizing our very existence as Jews. We thought Hitler was crazy; now it seemed all of Germany was following his example. Where would it lead?

My family began to understand that we would have to get out of Germany, and my father was reconsidering the move to America. But leaving Germany was not so easy. We would have to first sell our house. But to whom? There were many preparations to be made, and the hostile environment slowed our progress.

There was also the fear that the house would be expropriated. The Nazi minister of economics, Walter Funk, once boasted that the Nazi

Party had managed to steal Jewish property worth two million marks by 1938 alone—all before the outbreak of war!

Often, family friends came over, always in secret, and tried to console us. Sometimes they said we did not need to leave. "Maybe Hitler won't stay around," they would say. "Maybe they will vote a new president in soon." But these were empty consolations; I could see that in my parents' faces. Hitler was not to prove the kind of man who would ever let go of power—on the contrary, he would try to grow his power base and lead Germany into another worldwide war.

My parents' friends then suggested that maybe Hitler would be deposed. Some said he was a tyrant, that he was unpopular and that he breached the laws of the state by declaring himself supreme leader. They said how could such a man stay head of the state in Germany, a civilized country?

But who then were these people in the streets cheering his name? Who comprised the great masses screaming, "Sieg heil!" ("Hail victory!")? Did our family friends really believe Hitler was so unpopular among the German people to whom he had promised Germany would be returned to a position of global prominence? He seemed rather popular to us.

More than once, we wondered if the same people coming in secret to comfort us were not also out in the crowds by day, cheering and chanting Hitler's name. It seemed unthinkable, but what about the world then, was it not unthinkable? Germany was a civilized country, one of the most advanced countries in the world, and yet it was ruled by a despot. We too didn't understand how he could stay in power, but with more and more people shouting "Heil Hitler!" in the streets every day, how could we ignore that? We could not. Hitler would not allow it!

No, we knew it was bad for Jews, and it would only get worse. By 1935, my family's idle thoughts of leaving the country began to coalesce into definite plans. We were driven by a deteriorating situation that could no longer be ignored.

In 1935, two signs were placed on opposite sides of Barsinghausen. One read, "For Jews, there is nothing here to be earned." The second sign had an even more ominous inscription: "Jews enter this place at their own risk." While the latter sign was taken down after just a short time, our memory of it remained. The *Eckerde District Chronicle* of Barsinghausen reported that the signs were meant to "educate the people about the spiritual and physical danger of this alien race." What danger were we? We didn't know.

What we did know is that it was time to get out of Germany. We worried about what would become of us if we stayed. We didn't yet suspect the horror ahead that would face those who stayed behind—how could we have imagined what was to come? —but we were very concerned with the political instability and the growing anti-Semitism. People had begun to vandalize my father's store, painting anti-Semitic caricatures and phrases onto the windows with dirt.

The time to go was now, but until we could go, we needed to protect ourselves. We hatched a plan to do so: we would assume Polish nationality. My father was Polish, which allowed him to acquire Polish papers. The hope was that we would be protected as foreigners.

We thought that this plan would keep our property from being seized by the state or anything else from happening. Mostly though, we hoped it would buy us some time while we tried to sell the house and make other preparations for our departure from Germany. My father had lost much business at his tailor shop because many people no longer wanted to patronize a Jewish business; others did not want to be seen doing so. We were financially ruined. My father had to slash his prices just to retain his last few customers. The few that still came did so because they could get suits tailored for far less than they would pay at other shops run by non-Jews. Despite the business being shattered, we did still bring in enough money to be able to live off the proceeds, albeit at a much lower standard of living than we were accustomed to, which bought us time to plan our departure.

What was that plan? We didn't quite know. It was decided that Rosa should go to Hanover for a milliner's apprenticeship, learning to make and sell women's hats so that she might start a business like our father's. We believed she would be safe there—a young girl in the tutelage of a tradesperson and out of our father's household. No one would have to know that her father was Jewish. Because I was still a child, I would go with my parents to Poland.

My mother was not in a hurry to leave her birthplace and family. All her parents and siblings were in Germany, and her whole life was there. I felt very bad for her, but what could we do? She was married to a Jewish man, she had Jewish children, and she herself had converted.

Between 1936 and 1938, we were ever more eager to get out of Germany. More anti-Semitic laws were passed every day, such as requiring Jews to adopt "traditionally Jewish" names so that they would be easily recognizable as Jews. We started to worry we might never be able to get out. On October 5, 1938, Jewish passports were invalidated, including our own, and replaced by those marked *J* for Jew. We worried about what this marking meant. In hindsight, of course, it was clear they were already cataloging and tagging Jews for later extermination or deportation.

We wanted to leave, but we simply didn't know where to go. Some had fled to Palestine, present-day Israel, but this was no longer possible. It was a territory of England at the time, which, like most countries, was keeping its territories closed to Jewish migrants. Many modern-day Americans and other people who didn't live through those days have the misconception that anti-Semitism was limited to Germany. This was far from the truth. Anti-Jewish hysteria had spread across Europe and the globe: no one wanted to take us in.

We longed to go to America, but we weren't allowed to. My father tried to secure visas, but the Polish quota had been exceeded. They told us we would have to wait eleven years to go. Eleven whole years! We didn't have eleven years. As bad as things were getting, we weren't so sure we even had eleven weeks. Applying for Polish citizenship, originally a safety measure, had backfired—not only were we not safe in Germany, but we also could not go to America because of our Polish citizenship.

We then tried to apply to go to America under the German quota. My mother, sister (fig. 5B), and I were born in Germany and are natural Germans according to American laws, even if Germany didn't fully recognize us. We went to the embassy in Hamburg to try, but the consul there was not agreeable. While we should have qualified, the consul blocked our attempts. They required my mother and her sisters to prove that they could support Rosa and me without the help of our father, who would not be able to go as a Polish citizen born in what had been Russian territory when he was born. Their request was denied, and we were stuck in Germany as things continued to get worse.

Figure 5B

CHAPTER THREE

SHATTERED GLASS, BROKEN FAMILY—KRISTALLNACHT AND MY DEPORTATION

O n the night of October 29, 1938, a hard knock sounded unexpectedly on our front door. When my parents answered the door, they were greeted coldly by a municipal employee, a man I will call SH, and three policemen. They told us that we were all under arrest and that we were being deported to Poland. The reason? Our father was a Jew born outside of this country. My father tried to argue, but having applied for Polish citizenship, he didn't have a leg to stand on with the officers. Not that it would have mattered—they were not deporting him for his citizenship status. They were deporting him for being Jewish. We would share his fate. All this passport nonsense was mere pretense.

I was asleep in my bed when the SS officers arrived. My father came into my room to wake me, but I was already up. I had heard sobbing—my mother crying in the other room—and the cold voices of the SS officers.

"Get dressed," my father told me.

"Why? I must go to school tomorrow."

"No, we have to go," he said.

"I can't go!" I protested. I had just finished my homework and stacked it neatly on a table in my room. I had to be at school early the next day to hand it in to the teacher. A poor naïve child.

The intruders did not care about my homework, of course. I could hear them in the other room telling us all to get dressed and quickly pack our things. "You're going to Poland!"

"My mother too?" I asked.

"Yes, she has a Polish passport!" they said coldly.

My mother continued crying. "At least leave me here with the children!" she said, addressing SH. "After all, you are a friend of my brother-in-law, Wilhelm Ernst. You know my children and I were born here! We have never even seen Poland, why must we go there? Let us stay here!"

Her appeals fell on deaf ears. Either they did not care or they understood there was nothing they could do. Our personal history with this man SH meant nothing now, not in Nazi Germany. All that mattered was that we were Jews. They told us to grab our passports, the new ones marked with a *J*, and gave us only a few minutes to pack our bags. At least they let us pack our bags—we would find out later that many others were not so lucky.

When people think of the Holocaust, they likely think of Germany as the primary perpetrator. It is true that Germany instigated and carried out much of the anti-Semitism, but they are not the only guilty party. Poland also participated in the anti-Semitic orgy.

Sentiment toward Jews there was almost as bad as in Germany. On October 6, 1938, the Polish government revoked all Polish passports if their bearers had lived abroad for more than five years, specifically targeting Jewish Poles to keep them from fleeing Germany to Poland, as many had been doing. The order went into effect on October 31 of the same year and would mean that fifteen thousand Polish Jews living in Germany would lose their Polish citizenship on the last day of October.

This was unacceptable to the Nazi Party. They did not want to be stuck with fifteen thousand stateless Jews, including my father, with no place else to go. It was clear that no other countries were going to take us off their hands.

The Polish government did not announce the decision to prevent Jews from coming back. However, Germany took the matter into its own hands and informed Poland that if the law went through,

Germany would deport the Jews immediately. Poland did not concede, and Germany followed through on October 27, 1938. They announced that some twenty thousand Jewish people and their families would be rounded up and taken by train to Poland within forty-eight hours to get them back to Poland before the October 31 deadline.

Of course, we knew nothing of these plans until the last moment.

We were all escorted out of our house in the middle of the night and taken to the police station. They then took us to a building situated at Burgstrasse 28/29 in Hanover. The building had previously been administrative offices for a printers' trade group, but in October 1933, the National Socialists named the building Rusthaus ("Rust House") after Bernhard Rust, the National Socialist minister of Science, Education, and National Culture. This esteemed building was now to be used for a nefarious purpose: as a holding station for Polish Jews, people like us, that were to be deported to Poland.

Rusthaus was not the only such station. There were five hundred people with us that day, but the same thing was happening across Germany though we did not know that at the time. More than twenty thousand German Jews were taken from their homes on the nights between October 27 and 29, 1938.

By the time we arrived at Rusthaus, hundreds of Jews were already there, under the merciless watch of the police, the SS, and the Gestapo. The Gestapo inspected our papers. We stood there waiting, biting our nails in anticipation. We didn't know what would happen. Finally, the Gestapo told us that my mother, my sister, and I could return home—it was only my father that had to be deported. He hugged us goodbye and kissed my mother. We started to depart, leaving my father behind to an unknown fate.

My mother took us by the hand and walked us away, slowly at first, then picking up pace. We were about to make our exit when one of the officers chased after us, shouting at us to stop, to wait. They told my mother they had changed their minds, that there had been an error. She could still go, but my sister and I had to stay; we too would be deported to Poland, presumably since our father was Jewish.

My mother was desperate to stop them from taking us from her. She called out to my father, "What should I do now?"

My father shouted back, struggling to be heard from so far away. "Lina, go back home to Barsinghausen! You still must feed the animals. At least one of us will be in the house!" He tried to sound reassuring.

Tears filled my mother's eyes as she looked at us and then at our father in the distance. The Gestapo stood there, looking impatient and menacing.

She looked frantic. She did not have time to mull over her next action—the Gestapos were reaching for us. Should she try to make a run for it with us? That would be impossible with all the armed guards and soldiers around. Rosa and especially I would not have been able to outrun the soldiers, even if there were a safe place to run to. But there was no safe place in the world for us, most of all in Germany. Deportation was beginning to sound like a good thing!

My mother also had to think fast because there was a very real chance that she herself could still be detained. I could tell she was weighing that possibility. Would it be better to be detained and stay with her children? Or if the whole family was deported to Poland together? Or should she remain behind and watch the house, maybe sell the house before officials seized it, and then join us in Poland?

I saw all of this on her face even though it was a mere flash—but the moment seemed to go on forever. Finally, my mother yielded. She told us to go with the Gestapo, to rejoin our father, and to stick close to him.

My mother later told me that she had waited outside for many hours, just standing there waiting and crying with a heavy heart. She was waiting to see if we would emerge from the building—perhaps, she thought, they will still let the children go? But no, it did not happen. No one emerged from the building, though more people and families were brought in. But the only people that emerged from the facility were the Gestapo and guards coming and going, ushering in other families.

Eventually, after much time, she gathered herself and returned to Barsinghausen. Our house waited for her there, empty.

Imagine what my mother went through the moment she lost sight of my father, my sister, and me at the Rusthaus. You're suddenly alone. Three quadrants of your heart have vanished, and the remaining piece of your heart is broken. You cannot feel the bitter November wind as you walk blindly along familiar streets back to a house that is no longer a home because it is devoid of family. Every corner of every room echoes with the voices of the children and a husband you may never see again. But you cannot leave this place. Here in this husk of a home you must remain, waiting in the hope that they will someday return.

Meanwhile, we were held inside the facility, waiting to see what would become of us. We knew we were to be sent to Poland; but we did not know how, when, or for that matter, *why*.

They transferred us to a different room, an old gymnasium. The gymnasium was a large bare room with a wooden floor, not a secondary school where students were preparing for university. Unbeknownst to us then, we were being held in the same place as the parents and siblings of Herschel Grynszpan, the Polish Jewish refugee who would be blamed for setting off the atrocities to follow.

When Grynszpan heard about his family's deportation in the following weeks, he lashed out at the German state by assassinating Ernst vom Rath, a Nazi diplomat, in Paris. The Nazis used this assassination to set off the so-called Kristallnacht ("Night of the Broken Glass"), a series of coordinated state-led attacks against Jews living in Germany. The night is named for the sounds that rang out as German officers broke the windows of Jewish shops, homes, and synagogues. This event set off the Holocaust as it is known today. Ninety Jews were murdered that night. Thirty thousand more were arrested and sent to the first mass concentration camps. Grynszpan was a convenient scapegoat for the Nazis. Without him, the German government would have found another way to justify the atrocities of Kristallnacht and set off the dominoes of successive horrors that fell rapidly from that point forward. To this day, I am astounded to have been caught up in such historic events. At the time, though, I was simply young, confused, and very scared.

The guards separated us into two groups, sending the men to one hall and the women and very small children to another. This is where we were separated from my sister. My father and I went one way, Rosa another. She looked frightened. My father was terribly sad, but he tried to reassure her that we would be close by in another room. Rosa was an adult, a young woman, but she was still very young and scared like all of us.

I waited quietly, staying close to my father, fearing that he and I would be separated next. More and more soon-to-be refugees were brought in. Some of them, like us, had baggage. Others were still in their pajamas, clearly having been taken there from their beds.

Why were some allowed to pack and others not? It was at the whim of the Gestapo. If you were unlucky, you were abducted and detained by the cruelest of the officers who would not even allow you proper clothes before forcing you out of the country. What everyone had in common, though, whether properly dressed or not, was a look of shock. Men, women, and children alike stood around weeping.

There was some small mercy. The police allowed coats from the Hanover Jewish Association to be distributed to those who didn't have any. Volunteers from among the abducted throng walked around and handed out coats to those in need.

Many SS officers came in and lined up along the wall. They had us line up on an opposing wall, and for a moment, it seemed almost as if they were preparing a firing squad. Thankfully, they were not. They told us to go and pick up our passports, which had been collected previously, and then return to our place, in order, along the wall. To do this, we had to pass the wall where the SS men were standing. The officers kicked and struck us as we passed for no other reason but torture. My father and I also had to run this gauntlet, being struck up and down the hall. I worried that somewhere nearby officers were doing the same to Rosa. These men were brutal hounds; they struck the elderly and children alike—such a disgraceful display that to this day I cannot believe it. I still cannot understand how the Third Reich had come to power, why they did what they did, or why the people tolerated it.

After we all had our passports and were lined back up, they loaded us into large police cars for detaining prisoners—they called these vehicles Green Augusts, which were large police vans that the officers used—and transported us to the train station for mass deportation.

From inside the police vehicles, we could watch our town and homeland zip by—the last time many of the transported would see their home. Groups of people stood on street corners. Some hurled hate-filled slogans with venomous tongues. These people were once our neighbors, but now they had turned on us in the name of this Third Reich. "Sieg

Heil!" some shouted. But not all of them. Others were different, we could tell. They looked remorseful, worried, sad. Some people had tears in their eyes as they watched us go by. But these were the few faces among many. There were already trains waiting at the station when we arrived. We were taken out of the police vans and loaded onto the train.

We looked for Rosa and, thankfully, found her. After reuniting, we took our place on the train, all three of us huddling into one compartment with many other people. There were also the police and the SS in the train cars too, guarding us but brutalizing us at times. People begged for water. We were so thirsty, having been offered no food or drink the entire time we were at the holding facility. Here too we were denied drink. I had never in my few short years on this earth ever been so thirsty.

We dozed off for a few hours on the train. I was thankful for sleep, to drift off into nightmares—at least they got me out of this real-world nightmare we were in! When we awoke six hours later, the train had stopped.

Crossing the Border

We were near the Polish border, in a place called Bentschen, where the customs station was. We were made to disembark the train and pass through customs.

The German customs officers asked us sarcastically, "Do you have anything to declare?" They thought this was very funny to ask the people still in their pajamas and nightgowns, carrying nothing but the coat on their backs.

The German officers warned us that it is against the law and severely punishable to bring more than ten reichsmarks over the border. We were very afraid of the threat of punishment—because what could be worse than what we were already experiencing? Some were so afraid that they gave away their few last marks before entering a foreign land where they knew no one, had nothing, and had no place to go.

We were again separated by gender, though small children were allowed to go with the women, regardless of gender. I was told to go with the men even though I was only thirteen years old. All male children over ten years of age were required to go with the men.

The women were loaded onto buses to be taken over the border into Poland. We, the men, had to walk. We gave our suitcases to Rosa to take on the bus. Single men had to carry their suitcases the long distance over the border if they had suitcases at all. The walk to the Polish border was a long trudge. It was six kilometers to the border, and many of those deported were not in good enough health to make the march—but they were forced to anyway.

We were divided into rows. The police and the SS walked behind us. The police, some of them, were not too unkind; but the SS, which we did not then realize was now the ultimate police power, was mostly cruel. They screamed at us to go faster the whole way even though many struggled with bags. "Faster, faster!" they barked.

Some of the walkers begged for a break. Those with suitcases were out of breath, their arms tired. There were many elderly. They dragged their bags behind them and struggled to keep up. The police seemed willing to allow for a break, but the military SS officers would have none of it.

"Come on, walk! Come on, faster!" the SS shouted at those who fell behind. They began to strike stragglers, even the old men who were completely exhausted from the weight of their bags. The SS snatched the bags from the hands of these stragglers and tossed them onto the ground, spilling their contents. These men, these unfortunate souls who were guilty of nothing but being older or weaker, were forced to leave their only remaining belongings behind.

At one point, I turned around and saw an old friend of my father, Mr. Pesses. He had two suitcases, one in each hand, and he carried another on his shoulders. He was out of breath, huffing and puffing, his face red. He paused and bent over. He could not go on, like so many of the others. Two SS men, beasts both of them, descended upon Mr. Pesses. One shoved the suitcase off his shoulders, cackling with laughter. The other snatched one of the suitcases from his hand and threw it to the ground, contents and all. "Now you can walk!" the SS officer snarled.

I turned back around and tugged at my father's sleeve to tell him what happened. "Dad, Dad," I said. "Mr. Pesses is back there!" My father tried to shush me, but I continued. "But, Dad, it's—"

I was cut off by a hard, dull impact to the back of my head that literally knocked me speechless. My eyes went momentarily out of focus. My head throbbed. My ears rang. An SS officer had struck me with his fist. My father could do nothing—it would have only made matters worse. What a thing it must have been for him to be unable to protect me. It goes against all natural parental and paternal instincts to accept that doing nothing was better than doing something. But he was wise to hold back, and his restraint *did* protect me because had he reacted, it's unlikely either of us would have made it to the border.

The SS officer pulled my school cap off and threw it to the ground. "Scorn of the German fatherland!" he shouted in my young face. Luckily, I was quick in those days. I darted away and disappeared into the crowd of trudging men. Once I was sure I had lost the SS officer, I began looking for my father. When I found him, he too was out of breath from the march to say anything about what had happened, and I was too concerned for him to mention it.

We marched on. I glanced back over my shoulder occasionally to make sure the officer who struck me before, or any of them, was not behind us. As far back as the eye could see was a trail of suitcases, fanning out behind us like a boat's wake. People had begun tossing their own suitcases voluntarily so that they could keep up. Having seen that stragglers were getting beaten, they wanted to avoid falling behind at all costs, even if it meant abandoning the last of their meager possessions along the German-Polish border, never to be retrieved. They were shedding the past behind them and marching toward an unknowable future, which for so many of them would be miserably short. They were right to be afraid. We were, after all, in a no-man's-land between Poland and Germany, a fragile border that would mean nothing mere months later when German tanks and troops would come pouring into Poland. We had no rights here in this nowhere place, not as far as these thugs were concerned. They could do whatever they wanted with us, so we tried to keep in line.

The memory of the entire march has stuck with me since that day, but even now, seventy-five years later, one image remains so clear it is as if it happened only a few minutes ago.

There was a Jewish man about seventy years old. He carried nothing with him except his prayer shawl and his prayer book. He kept his book, as many did, in the iconic velvet prayer box. There was a Star of David embroidered on the front of it. He clutched this box firmly under his arm as he marched, tucked between his arm and body so as not to lose it. But he was elderly and in poor health, and he struggled to keep up with the pack. The SS were on his heels, shouting, "Move along faster, old man!" Finally, when the man could go no more, two SS officers came up behind him and seized him by his arms. The Jewish man's feet dragged behind him as the two officers pulled him along, but this man of faith and culture never let go of his bible and prayer shawl.

I will always remember that image of those two barbarians dragging a proud elderly believer out of the country, away from his home and family, away from everything he had known. Despite his abuse, this man lost neither his dignity nor his faith, and I hope that he was able to keep hold of those, even if he ultimately lost his life in the next few years.

When we neared the border, more SS officers appeared, and other regular German soldiers were waiting for us. They were everywhere. The border fence was visible in the distance, getting closer.

The officers and soldiers began shouting at us for standing around. "Go over there!" they shouted in German. "Go over there, to your stinking home. Go to stinking Poland! There's nothing for you here. If you come back to Germany, you'll be shot!"

We rushed through the border fence quickly. We were glad to be out of the "civilized" country and happy to be in "stinking Poland."

Yet when we crossed over into Poland and reconnected with Rosa, who was waiting for us with our suitcases and the rest of the deported women, we soon discovered we were not wanted there either. There were only a few border guards on the Polish side. They seemed puzzled as to why we were there, and they were not welcoming. They sent us on to the next town of Zbaszyn.

And so it was that I entered Poland, a thirteen-year-old refugee.

CHAPTER FOUR

GAME OF HOT POTATO—
BEING AN UNWANTED JEW IN POLAND

After years of trying to leave Germany, we had finally made it out—though not in the way we had hoped or imagined. Our own country, the country in which I was born but was no longer wanted, had exiled us. Our crime? Merely being Jewish. We were shocked, but not exactly surprised, given the situation in Germany.

We blamed Germany for kicking us out of our homes and were grateful that Poland was allowing Jewish refugees at a time when few countries were still accepting Jews.

When we got to the Polish side of the border, it was a relief to see how less militarized the border was. Whereas the German side was teeming with guards and soldiers and SS officers, the Polish side was relatively quiet with only a few guards. (At the time, this was a comfort; but in hindsight, it was probably a sign of the coming German invasion.) But when we disembarked the German trains and crossed into Poland, we were hopeful. We believed Poland was saving us.

Germany had carried out the operation at breakneck speed, deporting people in the middle of the night before Poland had time to react. The German's surprise strategy seemed to have worked, and it was understandable that the guards looked perplexed, but why did they look down upon us with such disgust?

It was then that our hope began to fade.

Never mind that most of the deported Jews were Polish citizens, like my father, or a family of Polish citizens, like my sister and I. Our nationality was secondary to our cultural heritage: Poland clearly did not want Jewish citizens returning to the country.

We got the feeling that they did not want to accept us but did not have a choice in the matter. We were, after all, Polish citizens, and the children of Polish citizens. We had even returned to Poland before the November 1 deadline that would have robbed us of our citizenship. They had to let us in!

We waited while the German police negotiated with the Polish officers. Eventually, a deal was struck, or an understanding was reached, and we were allowed to enter the country. The Germans began loading our suitcases onto horse carriages, which were then to be dispatched to barracks on the border where they would be returned to their owners.

We first met up with the women who had crossed the border by bus. My father and I searched frantically for Rosa. We were relieved to find her safe among the other women and children. She still had our suitcases, which was also a relief because no one really knew if the Germans would actually collect and deliver the other suitcases as they had promised.

I thought again of the trail of suitcases that lay strewn across the border. I shuddered to think about it. We were lucky to have Rosa to carry ours for us; otherwise, we might have lost everything we owned— and there was very little left of it to lose. I thanked my sister for doing this for me, but of course, I would have done the same for her.

For their part, the Poles began moving people further into Poland by train. From the border, we were sent by train to Zbaszyn, the next town, which was where I would reside for much of the next year. It was a bewildering time in my life, a time of upheaval and uncertainty for both me and Jews everywhere in Europe.

I thought about how my father used to say that times were bad, but they had been worse. I now questioned whether he was right. I was young, barely a teenager, and so didn't have the vantage point that he had. But to me, both relatively and objectively, times seemed bad, worse than I had ever known them; and from the shadow on my father's face, it was clear he was beginning to rethink his previous position.

When we arrived in Zbaszyn, we were met with more Polish officers who did not know what to do with us. Hundreds and thousands of Jews were arriving by train from Germany with nowhere to go. Temporary accommodations were provided for us at the military barracks, a dilapidated complex. Initially, we were to be detained there only until they decided what to do with us, but as the days turned to weeks, it became increasingly clear that barracks would have to serve us on a long-term basis.

These accommodations were certainly less than we had been accustomed to at home in Germany. There were too many of us to fit inside the living quarters, and we were packed many to a room. Those who would not fit were quartered in a nearby stable. They stuck people wherever there was space, as many to a room as would fit. There were not nearly enough beds for everyone, so the Poles brought in straw for us to sleep on.

As bad as I make this sound now, things were better there than they had been in the detention center in Hanover or aboard the trains that had brought us to Poland. The guards were unpleasant, but they were, for the most part, not cruel and abusive like the Germans. They shouted at us, occasionally someone was struck, but there were no systematic beatings—no gauntlets to run like in the gym in Hanover.

There was more in the way of amenities too if you could call the basic necessities of life that. There was a water pump, so we had something to ease the parching thirst that had nearly killed so many people on the hot, crowded trains. That pump provided much-needed relief, but for the first few days, there was absolutely no food. Many people continued to go hungry unless they were lucky to have had the time and forethought to pack rations before the Germans whisked them away. There was no heating either, and we were heading for a cold winter.

Those first few days were very difficult. We didn't know how long we would be there or what the future held. We worried we would freeze or starve. We literally had nowhere to go, and we relied on the Poles for everything; they were both our caregivers and our captors. These men who did not much care for us—these were the people upon whom our lives depended.

It already felt like the world had turned against us; but soon, nature turned against us too as fall was exiled for another year by winter, the cruelest of all the seasons. Winter arrived in November, dark and malevolent, seemingly determined to torture us. We were ill-prepared and inadequately shielded from the elements. The windows of our dilapidated building had been broken out, and the wind and cold came rushing in at night. We had no blankets, just our straw mattresses, and we pressed into the coarse hay for what little warmth it could provide. The hay poked at my skin and made me itch, but I did not care about that: it was the biting cold that I hated. I was so cold that my teeth chattered, and my body shook at night from cold and malnourishment.

One night, I woke up to find my father was not at my side. I bolted up, startled by his absence until I realized he was sitting, shivering against the cold. I realized he had covered me with his coat. I will never forget this act, and I still cannot imagine what it must have been like for him to see his family suffer so much.

One cannot really understand that kind of cold and desperate hunger until one has experienced such deprivation. Even in these first few days, people began to succumb to the harsh living conditions. Each morning we would wake to hear of more elderly men and women who had died of exposure or disease the night before. The Poles would have to come in and take out the bodies, and the next night it would happen again.

This continued for three or four days, long enough for us to begin to wonder if we too would grow weak and die. Relief finally came in the form of a truck loaded with bread and butter from Posen. This was the first of many trucks that would come to bring the necessities we needed just to survive.

We had the Jewish Committee to thank for this relief. They had been trying for some time to distribute aid to the refugees, but the Polish government was slow to react to the Jewish diaspora. Only now had the Polish government granted them permission to help us. To this day, I cannot believe it took so many days for the Polish state to come to the aid of its own citizens, but that was how much the government loathed the Jews in its own land.

Thankfully for us, we had our fellow Jews look out for us. They took over relief aid and did what our Polish keepers would not—they provided food, basic medical care, blankets, and other necessities. On the first day that the Jewish Committee aid workers came, they handed out enough bread and butter for everyone. Ravenous, we consumed the food at speed, uncertain when our next meal would come. Our fellow Jews also distributed blankets so that we might not freeze to death. Now I could hunker down in blankets at night and no longer have to use my father's jacket to keep from freezing. It was the first night I was manageably cold. It still hurt my lungs to breathe in the cold air, causing me to cough and wheeze the night through, but at least my skin was protected.

The Jewish Committee rented a nearby house in Zbaszyn to use as a makeshift hospital. Volunteer Jewish doctors and nurses came from all around central Poland, mostly from Warsaw, to provide health care for the sick among us. This ended up being particularly fortuitous for me because all the cold nights sleeping in a barn and going around outside without a hat had made me ill. I had a terrible fever and sore throat from breathing in the cold air. My father rushed me to the makeshift hospital, where I was cared for by the all-volunteer medical staff. I fell very sick and became jaundiced. My skin was so sallow that the doctors were not sure I would make it, but I eventually pulled through. Was this hepatitis A or leptospirosis from contaminated water, I will never know. I remained in the hospital building for several days before I started to recover my health.

I wonder sometimes if I would have survived those days were it not for the volunteer doctors and nurses that the Jewish Committee brought in. It is very possible I would not have. That was my very first brush with death.

Mr. Cohen

For the first few weeks in Zbaszyn, the deported Jews remained in the barracks. Whether we were being simply quartered there or actually detained was a matter of debate because we were not free to leave the complex on our own. I certainly felt very much like a prisoner, and the experience was not wholly unlike my experience later in the Warsaw Ghetto.

The longer we stayed at the barracks, the more apparent it became to the Poles that we would not be allowed to return home to Germany anytime soon, if ever. Therefore, they began redistributing the refugees throughout the town, matching us with local residents willing to serve as hosts. This was not an easy task, as the people of the town were very poor and had little to offer except slightly more space and windowpanes that were not lying shattered on the floor. The process of finding suitable hosts was slow. Often, it was up to us to find our own hosts, which took time and effort. Many people had no interest in helping. Some did not even want us in their town. Others simply didn't have the money, space, or resources to take us in. Despite the challenge, my father persisted in trying to find us a better place to stay.

A few days after being released from the hospital, I was introduced to a man my father found to take me in, an eighty-year-old Jewish man by the name of Mr. Cohen, who had been living all alone in his house. Now Mr. Cohen had taken in many other people as well even though his house was modest and did not have enough beds for all his guests.

I was happy with the move my first night in his house, even if it was nearly as crowded as the barracks. It was nice to be away from the Polish guards and in the home of this generous Jewish man. We still had to sleep on straw, many people to a room, but the rooms were heated and had windows, which was more than I could say for the barracks and the stables. Mr. Cohen did not have enough space for both my father and me, so my father was forced to remain at the barracks while he continued to look for another host. I visited him there often and returned home at night to stay with Mr. Cohen.

Fortunately for my father, the conditions at the camp continued to improve, thanks to the Jewish Committee. They were now arranging the distribution of warm meals, and sometimes I would eat there with my father before going back to the house. They rented out buildings in the area—such as schools, mills, and houses—where food could be cooked and distributed for free. It was a strange life, but with all the fellowship, it was feeling more manageable.

Despite the help of the Jewish Committee, things remained very hard and perilous for us. After just a few days of living at Mr. Cohen's house, I again fell ill with a fever. Mr. Cohen informed my father, who rushed me back to the makeshift hospital. I had only been out a week or so, and there I was in a hospital bed again. That is how deplorable our conditions were; you could get sick and die at the drop of a hat due to the cold and disease and malnourishment. I stayed in the hospital for several more days, miserable with a fever, chills, and sweats. My throat ached and burned. My father worried for me, fearful that I might catch pneumonia and not recover.

I did recover, eventually. By the time I was healthy and strong enough to leave the hospital this second time, more changes were afoot at the camp. My sister was no longer at the camp in Zbaszyn. She was no longer in town at all, and my father told me that fifty children and teenagers had been allowed to go to central Poland. Rosa was among them.

I was extremely sad that my sister was gone but relieved she had gotten away from there. I did not like her sleeping on hay and going to sleep cold and hungry every night. She was safe with her family now. My father's sister lived in Skierniewice ("Ski-ern-ie-wice"), a town near the capital of Warsaw, which was where my sister had gone. Our cousin was there too. Our paternal grandparents had passed away a few years earlier, but our aunt still had a house there. I was jealous of Rosa for being able to stay with family, where I believed it was safe, but I was also happy for her. I wanted so badly to join her. My illness had ruined my chances of an escape, and I was sad about that, but my father would not have been allowed to leave also. I would not have been content to leave him all alone, so perhaps my illness was a blessing.

So my father and I remained in Zbaszyn, my father at the barracks and me with Mr. Cohen. We were hoping to find a host who could accept both of us so that we would not remain separated. But the process of finding hosts remained slow, despite my father's best efforts.

This changed suddenly when the Jewish Committee began offering prospective hosts fifty groszy (half a zloty) per day for each person they took in. This was not much even then, but in a small town with only six thousand residents and few jobs that paid a wage, any income was welcome. The refugees had been a burden to the townspeople, but suddenly, we were a source of real income; and in a matter of days, every refugee had found a suitable host, including my father and me.

Together Again

My father and I were finally able to sleep under the same roof once again. I no longer recall his name, but our new host was the town's *lichtanzuender*—the person responsible for lighting the gas lamps that kept the town illuminated at night. This was before electricity had come to all the small towns in Europe. Every evening, he went around town lighting each lamp by hand.

The house we stayed in had only two rooms, but our host had taken in four people. This was fewer than Mr. Cohen had taken in, but it was not ideal. We slept all in the one extra room. My father and I shared one bed while a woman and her daughter took another pushed up against the opposite wall. At night, we could hear each other's breathing and snoring. My mother and sister had been replaced by two women who were unknown to us. How odd to be living so close together, as close as a family unit, and yet be perfect strangers. I do not remember their names or know what became of them, and yet, for a time, we were living so intimately in a home that did not belong to us. It was to be a situation that was strange at the time but one I would become very accustomed to.

As far removed as this life was from our lives back in Barsinghausen, the accommodations were better than what we had suffered through over the past few weeks. We began to enjoy more freedom as well. We were no longer under the constant watch of the barrack guards, so we felt a little less like prisoners.

However, do not let me understate the case: we were neither free nor living with any dignity or justice. And we were still very much prisoners. We were sometimes freer to go about town now, but we were not allowed to leave. The Polish military guarded the roads leading out of town as well as the train station to keep us from disappearing into the country while they decided what to do with us.

How could you describe us as anything but captive? There was no escape—not that we had anywhere to escape to. My mother was still back home in Barsinghausen, but we could not hope to return there safely, even if we had managed to escape. We had to remain and wait and wait. And wait.

My father and I remained in Zbaszyn through the winter. We made it through alive, thanks mostly to our host and the Jewish Committee, to whom I am forever thankful and indebted.

The months ticked by slowly, and it was so very cold. But finally, spring came to Poland and the land began to thaw, the trees and fields began to turn green, and the nights were not quite so cold.

A Glimmer of Hope: A Return to Germany

May ushered in more than just fresh foliage and warmer weather—it also brought with it big news. We were informed by the Poles that Jews with property in Germany would be allowed to return to liquidate their property and assets. The Germans were going to let us return to our homes if only long enough to sell them. What to make of this? On one hand, they were clearly trying to strip us of our property, but on the other, we would at least be able to sell the house, as well as my grandparents' old house. My father hoped to make enough money from the sales to carry us through these tough times and maybe to America or anywhere safer than where we were.

Later, we learned that this situation was the result of a negotiation between the Poles and the Germans. As you might guess, the mutually agreed arrangement was not as rooted in benevolence as we would have hoped for. The Germans were not allowing my father to sell up out of any sympathy for our plight or suffering; Germany simply wished to rid their country of Jewish property owners. For Poland's part, they hoped to skim money off the top of the transactions. My father suspected this at the time, but what could he do? He had to at least try to get money for the house. It was our only hope. We owned nothing else. Furthermore, my father was desperate to return to see his wife.

We had heard early in the process that many were using the opportunity to escape Europe. Because family members were allowed to accompany the property owner, many of the Jewish families who returned to Germany took advantage of this fact, selling off their assets quickly and immediately going elsewhere. Some went to Bolivia, some to the Dominican Republic, and others to Shanghai. These were some of the few places that were still accepting Jewish refugees at the time. Most places would not have us, including the United States, which had imposed strict quotas on Jewish immigration.

Germany allowed deported Jews back in for liquidation in measured phases. Unfortunately for us, this was done by alphabetical order, and Weiss was one of the last names on the list.

It was not until late May that we finally got word it was our turn. By this time, Germany and Poland had gotten wise to the Jews who were taking the money and fleeing. To prevent this, the Germans no longer allowed family members to accompany the property owner to Germany, and both countries cracked down on people trying to flee with liquidated assets. Poland and Germany wanted their share of the proceeds.

So, in May 1939, Adolf Weiss, my father, packed his few belongings into his suitcase and headed back to Germany. It would be the first time in over half a year that we were to be apart but the first time he would see his wife and step foot inside his own house again.

Luckily, I did not have to stay in Zbaszyn by myself. The Poles agreed to release me from detainment. Since my father was leaving, I was to go to live with Rosa. After she had left us in Zbaszyn, my sister had become engaged to a man by the name of Pinie Grayek, and this man was coming down to Zbaszyn to pick me up and take me back to my aunt's house in Skierniewice (fig. 6A).

Figure 6A

I was glad to be staying with a host and no longer living in the camp by the time my sister's fiancé came to pick me up. I would have been embarrassed by the conditions in which we were living and wouldn't have wanted to subject him to such a picture of misery as we had endured in the Zbaszyn camp. To have my future brother-in-law see our family sleeping on straw, dozens to a room, well, I wanted no association with such a place. Excited and hopeful, I traveled with Pinie to Posen, where we met up with his friend Jidel, a family friend. From there, the three of us traveled together to Skierniewice to be united with my sister and my cousin, Shimon.

I remember my arrival in Skierniewice clearly now, eight decades later. We arrived at the big redbrick central station, the size of which was a bit of culture shock after living in a small town for so long. It was evening when we arrived, and the weather was that of a mild summer. The memory of winter and the cold stables were wonderfully distant. At the station, I was surprised to see young men with beards and curly sideburns (*payot*) wearing black gowns and little caps. I asked my future brother-in-law, "What's going on here, a masquerade?"

He laughed and said, "This is how our pious people dress. This is normal here. It's just how they live."

I had never seen Orthodox Jews. Certainly, we would not go about dressed as such in Germany—it would not have been safe, so it was all new to me.

First, we went to my aunt's house in town. My uncle was a droshky driver, meaning that he owned a horse taxi. He had two coaches and three horses in the yard and a stable out back. These provided him and his family with a modest, honest living and allowed him to lead a comfortable and happy life.

The house had only a kitchen and two other rooms—a living room and one bedroom, though people slept in both. The ceiling leaked in the bedroom. When it rained, we had to place buckets beneath to catch the droplets. There was another bed in the kitchen with a straw mattress, where my uncle's deaf-mute son from his first marriage slept.

Skierniewice would be my home for the next two years. Mostly what I remember is being overjoyed to be with Rosa, Pinie, Shimon, and so many other family members. The familiar faces of loved ones warmed my soul like nothing had in the previous six months and like nothing would again for many years to come.

For my father, things were not as happy.

Meanwhile, in Barsinghausen ...

The liquidation process should have been simple, if not joyous; but in the end, it was neither. My father planned to sell our house in Barsinghausen, as well as his father's house up the street, and both houses would fetch a good amount of money on which we could live or, if we were lucky, escape. Our house was sold quickly to a German man, but when my father went to withdraw the money from the bank, he discovered that the money had already been confiscated by the Nazi State.

My father had feared this would happen, but there had been no choice but to go through with the liquidation of the houses and hope for the best, knowing that likely those hopes would be dashed. This, surely, had been the Nazi plan all along—to rob the Jews first of their houses and then their money (and ultimately of their very lives). Now it was confirmed: we were now without both homeland and home.

My parents were at a loss as to what to do next. Where would they go? How would they get there with no money? How would they live? How would they take care of their young son? How would they keep their soon-to-be-married daughter safe? What should they *do*?

I do not know the content of their conversations. I imagine the discussions were painful and confusing—at best based on hope and determination and at worst based on fear and despondency. How can you make rational decisions in a world that seemed so illogical? Nothing that was happening made any sense, so there could be no "sensible" decisions. At this terrifying crossroads, my mother and father simply had to choose a path, knowing whichever route they took would be arduous and dangerous and there would be no turning back. They knew each road would be tough, but they could not have known then what we all know now: that each road would be paved with ash that could lead any one of us to different versions of the same hell: Auschwitz, Treblinka, Dachau, Bergen-Belsen, Buchenwald, Belzec ...

My mother was not Jewish and so could stay in Germany without fear for her life. If she accompanied my father anywhere, she might have been subjected to the same discrimination. And so, in the end, my parents' decision was that my mother would not join us in Skierniewice. She would stay behind in Barsinghausen and take a job as a seamstress for a garment factory. She was able to work out an arrangement with Mr. Brandt, the man who had bought our house—our stolen house—that allowed her to live in a small room in the attic. In addition to her job at the garment factory, she spent nights and weekends weaving wreaths for Mr. Brandt. He sold these to the cemetery. My mother was paid just eleven cents an hour and given "free" lodgings in the house that was rightfully hers.

When I think of it now, I am still outraged. I want to believe Mr. Brandt felt bad for having taken the house and that was why he allowed her to stay, but he should have given us our house back. It was not right. The reality is that he and others like him stood to gain from Jewish losses, and greed trumps kindness all too often then and now. The positive side to this arrangement was that my mother was able to remain safely in Germany for the rest of the war and never had to endure the terrible ghettos in Poland.

So, my mother stayed in the one room in the attic of our house while my father returned to Poland alone. He was not allowed to stay at the house, nor was he allowed to bring his children back to Germany. Even if Mr. Brandt had allowed it, to do so would not have been safe—we were Jews. Only my mother was safe in Germany. She had converted to Judaism upon marriage, but this was not reflected in her birth records.

Return to Poland

My father rejoined us in Poland, arriving in Skierniewice in the summer of 1939. He told us the tale of how the proceeds of the sale were confiscated by the Third Reich right away. We were, of course, heartbroken. The family was now flat broke.

We continued to stay with my aunt Cirel for a while, six people in one bedroom, but this was too much of a burden on her immediate family and hard on us as well. My father, therefore, had to figure out what our next step was. He still hoped to reunite the family again, including my mother in Germany, and travel to America together—but those plans would have to wait. There was no money. There was no way to leave.

In the meantime, my father began working as a tailor when he could, and he used the money to rent a small apartment in another house. We had no furniture, not much of anything, really, but it was our new home, and we were happy to be together. I quite enjoyed Skierniewice at the time. It was a strange new world to me, but I liked the people there and the town itself. (fig.6B)

Figure 6B

My future brother-in-law had three brothers, one of whom I got quite friendly with. He was about my age, and his name was Samuel. He had dark brown hair, a long skinny face, and a good sense of humor. He became a good friend in town, and we spent a lot of time together. He introduced me to his friends and other young people around town, and I made friends. At night, we went to the movies and to the marketplace. That's how life was in Poland that summer. It was warm and peaceful, and there was family. It was a good time in my life, that summer. Things had returned to some semblance of normal although the separation from my mother was a constant source of pain.

But the calm was short-lived. Two months later, bombs began to fall on Warsaw, which was only an hour's drive from Skierniewice. We could hear them going off in the distance. We saw the German bombers fly over us in formation on their way to the big city. Skierniewice was bombed too, as were the other surrounding villages. And soon German soldiers and tanks came pouring into Poland. It was September 1, 1939. Hitler had invaded Poland, and World War II had officially begun.

CHAPTER FIVE

SHELTERING IN PLACE—THE WAR COMES TO TOWN

O ur life in Skierniewice had been some of the best days we had seen in many years since the beginning of the troubles in Europe. Unfortunately, those easy days were short-lived. Once Germany invaded Poland, things began to deteriorate, and much more quickly this time.

The night before the invasion, we heard bombs going off in the distance—the sound of German planes bombing railroads and other strategic points. The next day, they started bombing the town with low-flying planes. The planes flew close to the ground to attack. You could see the pilots' faces when they swooped down to unleash bombs or machine-gun fire. The extent of the bombing was hard to believe, like nothing that had been seen before in Europe or anywhere else. The industrialized carnage of the First World War had been a terrible sight to behold—but this was worse.

The Germans bombed rail lines.

They bombed factories.

They bombed houses.

They bombed cities and towns, soldiers, and civilians alike.

The Polish defenses were no match for the might of the German Army, and the smaller towns were the least defended. Skierniewice itself had little in the way of modern defenses to counter the German attack; there were a few antiaircraft machine guns, but nothing that could hope to fend off the onslaught of German fighter planes and bombers descending on the Polish forces: the Luftwaffe was an air force like nothing Europe had seen in action before.

From the ground, it was terrifying. As the first bombs began exploding near our house, panic broke out in the streets. Many houses and buildings were destroyed. The initial bombings went on for three days straight, much of it firebombing. We watched as Skierniewice burned around us and knew we could not stay.

Our family was living in a big stone house that we rented, newly constructed and beautiful. One day, Polish soldiers—wearing civilian clothes because they had no uniforms yet—knocked on our door and demanded to be let in and to stay. The soldiers had been staying in stores, but they now avoided them because the bombers were targeting those structures. Instead, they stayed with civilians, putting us at greater risk of being bombed!

But there was no truly safe place. The Germans bombed churches and stores and factories, any large building, and they had no qualms with bombing houses either. Their bombs gutted the house across the street from us. I watched its destruction from the window. The house didn't explode, not entirely, but it was heavily damaged. We ran out the doors and hid outside in case they bombed our house too. My sister was very terrified, but my father calmed her down, and we went back inside.

There was nowhere else to go—at least not in Skierniewice, so people began fleeing for Warsaw. It was believed that it would be safer there. Warsaw was a large city, and though it would surely be targeted by the Germans, it would also have much better defenses in comparison to the small towns. The hope was that the Poles would be able to keep the Germans from bombing the city or at least the houses.

This was a false hope, of course. We did not know how quickly and fully the German blitzkrieg would descend upon Poland. On the third day of the bombings in Skierniewice, we were at a neighbor's house when the radio broadcaster announced that England and France had declared war on Germany. We believed, naively, that the Stuka (German dive-bombers) would inflict their destruction and then retreat. We couldn't believe that Germany would face all of Europe and the rest of the world; we thought the war would be over quickly and that the Germans would fall back, and things would return to normal. We never imagined that Hitler would wage a multifront war against most of the industrialized world.

What we did not know in those first days was that German troops and tanks were already advancing through Poland, capturing cities as they went. We did not know about the Molotov-Ribbentrop Pact (also known as the Hitler-Stalin Pact), a nonaggression agreement between the Soviets and the Nazis that paved the way for the invasion of Poland. We did not know that in a mere three weeks, the Soviets would descend upon Poland from the East and that the country would fall even before France and England could mobilize.

These were the matters of politicians and military leaders, though. We heard rumors about these epic happenings, but on the ground, what mattered was daily survival. Like other Jews and Poles in Skierniewice, we resolved to flee to Warsaw, where we believed we would be safer behind the Polish front lines. We should maybe have known better—Warsaw may have had better defenses, but it was also a larger target of key tactical importance. Anyone who has seen pictures of Warsaw after the war knows it was all but leveled from bombing, first by the Germans and later by the Russians. The initial air raids lasted for a month, almost the entirety of September. In all, 85 percent of Warsaw was demolished by the end of the war, much of it in those first few weeks.

Whether or not we would be safe in Warsaw was something of a moot point. We did not know what else to do or where else to go. All we knew was that there were bombs falling on Skierniewice, and we did not want them falling on us. The Poles clearly could not defend the town with only a couple of horse-drawn machine guns and the Polish cavalry, not with hundreds of planes doing daily bombing runs. We told ourselves that we would figure out what to do in Warsaw once we got to Warsaw.

If only we had known what was to come, maybe we would not have gone.

CHAPTER SIX

WALKING TO WARSAW—OUR DOOMED SEARCH FOR SAFETY

With my father and sister, I set out for Warsaw on foot early in September, three days after the bombings started. The weather was beautiful and sunny—I remember that clearly, perhaps because of the stark contrast between the cheerful weather and the bleak events. We traveled in a pack of many other refugees. People brought only what they could carry, supplies and food, but even that was a burden. We moved slowly, so weighed down with supplies and misery. My father carried a bedcover strapped to his back. We brought a little food with us from the house, mostly dry goods.

The passage to Warsaw was not safe. It would not have been safe for us even before the war broke out, but things were worse now. We had to avoid aerial attacks, so we tried not to travel out in the open and to stay close to sheltered areas to protect us from a potential downpour of machine-gun fire.

It was impossible to always stay totally out of sight. We had to follow the roads to reach Warsaw. When the Germans spotted us, they would swoop low and open fire, sending us scattering. We would wait in the woods and in ditches for them to pass. They dropped bombs on the roads and civilian houses and killed Polish civilians in the fields and farms. These people were not even soldiers, yet the German army was killing them in their homes.

We stayed at farms along the way with whoever would take us in.

The first night, we stopped at a farmhouse not twelve miles outside of Skierniewice. The farm belonged to a Jewish man who took in refugees seeking temporary shelter. He didn't have much, but he shared what little he did have. The family gave us milk and something to eat. They were very friendly and kind, and we thanked them for the food and shelter.

My First Sight of Death

Despite the congeniality of the farmer, my father was uncomfortable staying at that farmhouse. With all the foot traffic coming in and out, he worried that the house would be targeted by bombers for housing refugees and possibly soldiers. Early the next morning, we packed our bags before breakfast and found a new place farther down the road.

My father's intuition would turn out to be prophetic. German planes came later that afternoon and bombed the first farmhouse. We had heard the planes coming, and counting several dozen, we scuttled for safety, taking refuge in a ditch in the woods. My father sheltered my sister and me with his body in case we were fired upon. My sister was very afraid; I could feel her trembling against me.

We were not fired upon, but the farmhouse we had stayed at had been. The planes rained down on the house with machine guns and dropped two bombs right on the place where we had been only a few hours earlier. The building exploded into flames. We did not emerge from our hiding place in the woods until all the planes were long gone, then we returned to help. Three men were wounded, and a mother and her small twin daughters were killed. The twins' bodies looked like little dolls in the field. These were the first casualties of war that I had seen—the first dead bodies I had ever seen in my life. It was a terrible sight; one I have not forgotten in over seventy years.

We continued our journey like this for several days, ducking into various farms along the way, staying wherever we could with whoever would have us. We were careful to avoid detection, though in truth there was little we could do to protect ourselves. We could have been captured or killed at any moment. We could have been bombed just like the people in the farmhouse. We were largely at the mercy of luck, and we hoped that luck would hold out.

On the fourth day of our flight from Skierniewice, we came upon a house in a forest just outside of a small village. There were other refugees housed there as well, but to our surprise, they were headed in the opposite direction. They were not headed to Warsaw but coming *from* there.

"You want to go to Warsaw?" they asked when my father told them that that was where we were headed. They looked sullen and despondent. "Turn back. We've just come from the main road from there. German tanks are already on their way to Warsaw. Go back, all is lost."

The color went out of my father's face. I felt numb to the news. This was not what we had expected. The radio, which we had been listening to regularly for updates, had not warned us that German troops were already in Warsaw. The other refugees traveling with us were also surprised. Everyone had expected England and France to have intervened before this.

The question was what to do now with this new information. If the Germans were in the middle of a land invasion, Warsaw would fall first, but they would eventually make their way to Skierniewice and the smaller cities as well. There was only one real option: we would have to turn around and return to Skierniewice. At least there we had a house in which to stay. If we were going to have to face German occupation, it was better to do it where we had a safe place to hide out.

Return to the Front Line

We started back to Skierniewice that same day. We were now walking into the war front instead of backing away from it; one could tell by the sound of gunfire and bombing. There were signs of Polish militarization everywhere. The Polish military was moving through the country, trying to organize a defense against the Nazi invaders. We passed many platoons along the way back to Skierniewice.

We understood that we would probably be stopped by the Poles at some point. They were less our enemies than the German military perhaps, but they were not our allies, at least not reliably. We had been treated unkindly by the Poles although, of course, much more cruelly by the Germans. But there were also many kind Poles who had helped us along the way, who gave us lodging as refugees. It was hard to tell if a Pole was a friend or foe to Jews, so we had to be careful whom we trusted.

Our group of refugees eventually found itself alongside a company of Polish soldiers with whom we merged. The Poles called us the "fifth convoy." When among the Poles, we were careful to speak little apart from Yiddish because it disguised our German accents. If we spoke German or Polish around the Poles, they would know we were from Germany, and we could be shot as spies. We could be killed for being Jews. We could be killed for being German. Truly it was a terrible position to be in.

A week had passed in the time it took us to make it back. When we reached Skierniewice, the Polish military stopped us. We were now very near the front line of the German invasion, and the Poles did not want us reentering the town, it being so close to the front. That night, we stayed in another farmhouse just outside of town. There were twenty people in a room, all of us lying closely packed on the floor like fresh sardines. By now, I was accustomed to such accommodations.

I was not so accustomed to the sounds of artillery and machine-gun fire in the night or the rumble of warplanes flying in formation. We could hear the Polish artillery firing into German lines and the sounds of firebombing in Skierniewice.

That night, the Polish troops retreated farther into Poland, falling back from even the outskirts of Skierniewice. When we woke the next morning, there was no one around to stop us from going into town. We packed our things and left the farm, thanking the farmers who had given us shelter. We returned to our house in Skierniewice, which was now in a no-man's-land. The Polish troops had gone; the German troops wouldn't arrive until later in the afternoon. The town was dead, the streets empty. Everyone had either already fled or was holed up in their homes waiting to see what would happen next. We did the latter. We locked the door, pulled the curtains closed, and waited to see what would ensue. We stayed indoors, hoping for the best, but fearing the worst.

Under German Rule Again

The Germans arrived later that day, riding into town in a motorcycle cavalcade. They took control of the town immediately with little resistance. The Polish forces had fallen back.

The Polish troops held out against the German advancement for a few more days after that, trying to hold their ground on the banks of the Bzura, a nearby river, before finally surrendering to capture. Some fifty thousand Polish soldiers were taken as prisoners of war and marched back into town by the Germans.

The Polish army had proved no match for the German forces. They were simply outgunned, and it wasn't just a matter of sheer numbers but of military technology. The Polish army was largely still using horse-driven vehicles to move artillery. They relied heavily on mounted cavalry. They stood no chance against the German panzer tanks that rolled into Poland. The Nazi soldiers were well armed, well supplied, and above all, supported by air forces. The Poles could simply not hold and withstand the constant aerial bombardment.

Poland never officially capitulated, but by October 8, 1939, the German Army had taken complete control of the country. Poland had fallen. The country was split in half and divided between Germany and the Soviet Union, the latter of which had invaded Poland under the pretext of defending Russian nationals, Ukrainians, and Belarusians, but really had done so as a land grab after the pact between Hitler and Stalin was enacted. Germany annexed western Poland, and the Soviet Union took the eastern half of the country.

What this meant for us, the Weiss family, was this: Skierniewice being in the western half, we were in German hands and at the "mercy" of the Third Reich once again.

CHAPTER SEVEN

CUTTING IN LINE—
SURVIVING THE GHETTO

The discrimination we had faced under German rule in Barsinghausen was nothing like what we faced now that the war was underway. The Nazis were now far less shy in their persecution of Jews in occupied Poland than they had been in the previous decade. Whereas before they had orchestrated the Kristallnacht as an excuse for mass deportations and offered excuses for freezing the bank accounts of Jewish citizens, they now cast aside any attempts to conceal their anti-Semitic intentions. Their intention to solve the "Jewish problem" was now out in the open even if the details and extent of the madness known as the "Final Solution" was yet to be revealed. It was all on the table now. If they wanted to do something to us or take something from us, they did not hesitate or make excuses.

The Nazis' first order of business in the annexed territory was to ransack all Jewish businesses. The Germans decreed that the Poles could rob the Jewish stores around the marketplace in Skierniewice. It was announced on the radio and over loudspeakers in town. Leaflets were distributed and signs posted. A bulletin displayed in town read something to the effect of "It's now free for everybody to go in the Jewish stores and take anything they want to." It was open season on our houses, our businesses, our personal property, and anything else we owned. Looting commenced immediately until every Jew in town had been stripped of all valuables they hadn't successfully managed to hide. The pillaging of our homes and shops went on for days.

As bad as it was in Skierniewice, things were worse elsewhere. There was rumor of atrocities transpiring elsewhere; unbeknownst to us, the genocide had already begun. Pinie had heard that ghettos had been formed in many of the neighboring towns, which were much more violent. Many Jews from there had fled to Warsaw only to turn around, much as we had. Unlike us, however, they returned to their hometown to find that every tenth man or so had been shot dead. Rumor had it (rumors that would later be confirmed into fact) that these executions were sanctioned by the German occupiers. In some places, the genocide had already started in earnest.

Fortunately for us, Skierniewice was still relatively calm and safe. The Germans gave the Poles explicit sanction to rob us, but they had not sanctioned murders—yet. That would come soon enough. Neither were we incarcerated in a ghetto, but that was imminent.

My First Ghetto

Once all the homes and businesses of the Jews in Skierniewice had been ransacked, the Germans began concentrating us in a single residential district designated for Jews. The same thing was happening across Nazi-controlled Europe.

The area of Skierniewice chosen for the ghetto had been home predominately to the Jewish community, but now we were *forced* to live there by proclamation and could not leave. Any Jews living outside of the ghetto were rounded up and relocated there by force immediately. Any non-Jews who had lived in the Jewish district prior to it becoming a ghetto quickly moved out due to the deplorable and unsafe conditions there.

Our family was among those forced from our home and relocated to the ghetto. We had to leave our new apartment and move into a blockhouse on the border of the ghetto, not far from the barracks, which was now occupied by the German troops.

Finding a decent place to live in the ghetto was hard. We managed to get a room in the blockhouse only because the owner and his wife, young people with a little bit of money, had fled to Soviet-held eastern Poland. Our entire family lived together in one small room in that house. There was a hole in the roof that we had to fix upon moving in to prevent rainwater from coming in. We had no furniture.

The Skierniewice ghetto, like most of the new Jewish ghettos, was "open" when it was first established. This meant that while we had to reside in the ghetto, we were still allowed to leave to visit the market and the business district. This meant that we could trade with the Poles easily, source supplies and food, and generally lead a normal life.

The ghetto, however, didn't remain open for long. Shortly after the ghetto was established, the German occupiers and the Polish puppet state decreed that Jews were no longer allowed to leave the boundaries of the ghetto for any reason, not even for emergencies. There was no recourse if you became ill or if your job was outside the ghetto. People were allowed to die sick and hungry in the ghetto.

I should stress that the ghettos, even the "closed" ghettos, were not concentration camps—this is a common misconception. The concentration camps were actual encampments, not community areas. There was a certain level of Jewish autonomy in the ghettos. Jewish bureaucracies sprang up. A Jewish council was formed to handle government administration. A Jewish police force was even established within the ghetto to keep the peace.

In the concentration camps, people were treated like slaves and workhorses—separated from their families, put to work, tortured, and often killed. But in the ghettos, families were at least allowed to stay together. We could rent apartments and have some semblance of a normal life. While it is true that people were murdered in some of the ghettos and many more succumbed to starvation and disease due to the conditions, the systemized and mechanized genocide that occurred in the camps did not occur in most of the ghettos, a small mercy.

Even after the ghetto in Skierniewice was closed, we could still move around inside the district, which functioned basically like a small neighborhood. Some areas were off-limits to Jews. They built a wooden bridge over the main street, for example, so that we could go back and forth between the two sides of the ghetto without setting foot on the main street. This was to prevent people from sneaking in and out. Sometimes we felt like we were in a chicken coop, but at least we could walk the side streets and go to the stores in the ghetto. We were relatively free to form our own Jewish community inside the ghetto. This was not true of the concentration camps.

Ghettos allowed families to live and work together and communities to form and function. But eventually, the Nazis would begin separating families and sending people to different concentration camps, and even death camps, but this would not start until later. In those early years of the war, we were allowed to stay together. This is ultimately what allowed us to survive those years and later escape Germany. We would have been hard-pressed to do either of those things alone. Without my father, I do not know if I would have made it. Actually, I do know I would not have made it.

All that said, the ghettos were not nice places, and I do not mean to downplay the role the ghettos played in Hitler's plans and in the Holocaust. I only mean to say that in the ghetto, for that time, life went on. We went about trying to make a living and trying to put food on the table. We worked, celebrated, and conversed. We held social gatherings. My sister and Pinie were even married while still in the Skierniewice ghetto. It was 1940. They held the ceremony in our apartment, and Pinie's grandfather officiated the wedding. It was a wedding celebration like any other—it just happened to take place in the ghetto.

We were in deplorable conditions, of course, and conditions continued to get worse and worse over time. We were always cold in the winter because there was no coal for heating. Instead, we burned wood that if we were lucky, we got from the Polish in exchange for clothes, furniture, money, and whatever little we had to trade.

By Whatever Means Necessary

The biggest concern, after having found an apartment to rent, was finding enough food to eat. This was a perpetual struggle for us. We were provided with little in the way of rations—barely enough food for a child to survive on, let alone a man. Not even close.

Luckily, we didn't have to depend solely on the daily rations as our only means of sustenance. If we had, we would have surely starved that first winter, every one of us, if we had not been able to buy food from the Poles. Stores had sprung up in the ghetto, and there was plenty of food—if you had the money. Many did not. Jewish businesses, homes, and bank accounts had been ransacked; and on top of that, inflation was out of control. Necessities were getting more expensive and scarcer with each passing day. The poorest among us simply couldn't afford to buy food from the Poles.

Our family was relatively fortunate. We did okay in the ghetto, all things considered. We seldom went without food. We were not having feasts, but we usually had something to eat each day. Our success was largely due to the fact that my father was a good tailor and businessman. My father made and sold suits to the Poles. The suits sold cheaply due to the wartime economy, but it was enough to get us by. My father sold one suit after another to bring money in.

Pinie and my sister also made money by selling sandals and shoes. Pinie came from a very wealthy family who had done quite well for themselves before the war by making fine leather uppers that they sold to different shoemakers across Germany and Europe. Now that the war was on and Pinie was in the ghetto, he took up this trade himself. They traded with the Poles for leather, which they made into shoes and sandals to sell back to the Poles. Their shoes were finely made and very popular, thanks to Pinie's great skill. Even Germans were coming into the ghetto to buy their shoes!

This is how we survived those years. We crafted and bartered and sold and recrafted and resold suits and shoes and whatever else we could for a profit. We did whatever we had to do to keep food on the table and wood in the oven to keep warm. We bought sacks of potatoes that we put down in the "cellar"—a hole under the apartment where we stored dry goods. We ate a lot of potato soup that first year.

With my father, Rosa, and Pinie working so hard, my contribution to the family was to stand in the food distribution lines to buy food. These lines were long, and there was no guarantee they wouldn't run out of what you wanted before it was your turn. I woke up very early to stand in line in the morning and would often have to stand in two or three lines a day.

Standing in the distribution lines could take five or six hours sometimes. My feet would start to hurt after a while, forcing me to shift my weight back and forth, back, and forth. It was worst in the winter. The cold would sting my face and make my fingers go numb. The winter of 1940 was particularly bitter; but there was nothing I could do but shove my hands into my pockets, hunker down against the cold, and wait. Sometimes one of the Polish farmers we bought food from would let me come into his home for tea and to warm up while we waited. But this was rare. Normally, I had to stand out in the cold like everyone else.

It was bad to be so cold, but it was worse to be hungry. Standing in line was what you had to do to survive, and so that's what I did; there was no way around it. I focused not on the cold or the pain in my feet, but on the hunger in my belly, on getting the things that we needed. Starvation is something few people in the West understand nowadays. Starvation is a different condition from hunger. Hunger has the taste of longing; starvation has the taste of fear—you can smell it on the breath of the people around you.

Standing in line was no guarantee you would get what you needed. Sometimes I would stand in bread lines for five hours waiting, able to smell the bread baking inside, and waiting for the bakers to emerge with loaves of warm bread, only to be told that they had sold out and to come back the next day. This happened more and more as time went on and supplies and food became scarce. It got to the point where lining up early in the morning was simply no guarantee that you would be able to buy anything at all. They would often run out early and turn people away empty-handed and empty-stomached.

Tough times called for tough measures. I learned a way of getting to the front of the line by watching other people. I am ashamed now to admit to having done this, but times were hard, and my family needed food. What I noticed was this: the strongest people would cut to the front of the line and simply claim that they were there first. Sometimes this would cause a fight to break out. The police often responded to these fights, but they were no real help. The stronger people who had pushed their way to the front simply claimed that they had been there first. It was one person's word against another's. The police didn't really care—they would just come in yelling, push people around a little, and leave once it was broken up. They didn't care who had cut in line.

This method of cutting to the front of the line worked well for me because I was young and strong and able-bodied. I'm not proud of this now, but we all had to do what we could to survive. I always left with what my family needed.

Despite the sometimes-cutthroat conditions we found ourselves in, the majority of Jewish people did their best to look out for their neighbors. We put ourselves and our immediate families first, yes, but the community was a close second. We gave to charity. We shared resources and information. We tried to treat our fellow Jews with the kindness no one else was showing us.

We tried to look out for each other the best we could, but there was only so much we could do for our fellow man given the situation we were all in. A Jewish community organization formed a soup kitchen to feed the poor. They accepted food donations from those who could give, though there were fewer and fewer who could as time wore on. There was also a place for people to donate clothes, blankets, coats, and shoes. These operations started strong but were stretched as the have-nots in the ghetto continued to increase. Money, food, and supplies became dangerously scarce. The longer the ghetto was cut off from the rest of the community, the worse conditions got. Every month, it seemed there was a new proclamation further restricting our movement to and from and within the ghetto. Every month, there was a new proclamation that stripped us of more basic human rights until it seemed that we had none left.

Surrounded

The first year was not so bad, but our situation began to deteriorate rapidly in the second year. In 1940, the Germans began building an enclosure around the ghetto. This marked a major turning point. Thus encircled, the ghetto began to feel less like a Jewish community and more like a Jewish prison.

We were still able to trade, but less food was coming into the Jewish district after the fences went up. Before, we had traded with the Poles who came to the ghetto. Now we had to trade through the enclosure. The makeshift fences were made of planks, chicken wire, and other scrap material, and we conducted business with the Poles through the gaps. But the more cut off we were from the rest of town, the less we had to trade.

It was hard to transact this way, but things could have still been worse. We heard rumors that the ghetto in Warsaw was surrounded by brick walls through which no trade could pass. We could only imagine how bad the conditions were there. They would have had to depend only on their meager rations, which weren't enough for anyone.

Trade became much more complicated and difficult. Before the enclosure went up, managing to find enough food was a constant but surmountable struggle. There had been goods and food for trading. There were materials for crafting things to sell and barter. We had been allowed to leave the ghetto to trade. One had been able to make a living, however limited, inside the ghetto. Only the very poor had had to resort to the soup kitchen that first year.

Now, fewer, and fewer people could afford what made it through the fences. We grew increasingly isolated and impoverished, my own family included. Trading now required Poles and Germans to come up to the fences, but fewer Poles and Germans were willing to trade in such an uncouth manner. This meant my father sold fewer suits. It meant that Rosa had trouble sourcing materials for leather and had a harder time finding buyers for her sandals and shoes. It meant that we had less money with which to buy food and wood for the fire.

Still, we managed to get by. Our father somehow managed to get a new sack of potatoes when the previous one went empty. There was always potato soup to eat—we just had to ration it more. My father had bought ten pounds of lard from a Polish man just before the wall was finished. We kept this fat in the cellar with the potatoes, using it sparingly.

Others were not so lucky. Many went hungry.

The enclosure also changed the general atmosphere in the ghetto. Now that the ghetto looked and felt more prisonlike, our captors took on a more oppressive air. They seemed more hostile and menacing. We used to go out into the streets often and freely, but we began to do this less and less. Mostly, we stayed at the apartment. This made for long, boring days. There were no schools in the ghetto, so my days were often long and empty as it was. Now I could no longer go out freely to see friends. I used to meet up with friends to play cards and chess but being out on the street began to feel unsafe. The Nazis would sometimes grab people off the streets and put them to work. Usually, they let them go at the end of the day, but the experience could be unsettling. It was safer just to stay in the apartment and be bored. Keeping us imprisoned must have been easy for the Nazis at this time; our own fears did a better job of keeping us inside our ghetto cells than any jailhouse guard.

I did still leave the apartment from time to time, just to walk the street or visit friends. I was not that afraid of living in the ghetto the way that Rosa was. In retrospect, I realize that this is because I never doubted that I would survive—not in the ghetto, not when traveling, not even when we were being shot at in the fields and on the road to Warsaw and back. Rosa was older. Rosa was now married, living in a honeymoon nightmare that threatened the shred of happiness she had found in falling in love. She now had someone else, besides me and my father, to worry about and fear for.

As a young teenager, you just don't consider the very real possibility that you will die. I didn't think about that, even in those days when death was all around us. My thoughts remained practical, mirroring my father's. I thought, *there is a war on. Poland is occupied by Germany. How do we get out? What do we do?* There was clearly no way to get out; we saw that on the road to Warsaw, and so instead we started asking ourselves how we would survive. In some sense, it was wrong to think this way: I could have died—many did. But this is not how I thought while in the thick of it. Perhaps I knew on an instinctive level that it was best to be optimistic and have faith. While hope was gone for so many in other situations, all was not yet lost for us in the ghetto, so it seemed the right thing to do was to think positive thoughts.

A Mother's Lifeline

As making money in the ghetto became ever harder, we relied more and more on valuables and money sent to us from my mother. She regularly shipped us care packages from Germany. Surprisingly, the mail was still being delivered to the ghetto. She sent us all kinds of things to barter. She sent clothes mostly, old clothes and things she had sewn at the factory. She sent anything we could use, sell, or trade.

She also sent money, but the money had to be disguised to prevent theft; you never knew who might be going through your mail. My mother would bake five marks into a cake and mail it to us.

Some of this money came from her job at the sewing business factory where she worked. Some of it came from the sale of our house, which had given her some income. (While the Germans had not let us withdraw most of the money, there was a short period during which she had been able to withdraw two hundred marks a week from her account. The account was eventually frozen, and the money all stolen, but she had squirreled away the two hundred marks a week for as long as she could.)

Though I did not know it at the time, I later discovered that she had also taken to begging on the streets of Barsinghausen in order to buy things to send us. I do not like to think of my mother begging, especially on my behalf, but I am not ashamed to admit that the help from my mother was very important. Her sacrifices were crucial to our survival, especially once they built a wall around the ghetto. Without her, I might not be here today. I am beyond thankful to her, as well as my father, for helping the family make it through those very tough years.

As hard as it was, we were surviving. We spent just over a year in the Skierniewice ghetto, from October 1939 until early 1941. We managed to make a life for ourselves as we waited out the war. Then in 1941, we began hearing rumors that Jews in Skierniewice would be relocated to the Warsaw ghetto, notorious for its poor conditions. No food. Rampant disease. Worse, we had also begun to hear rumors of the concentration camps being set up throughout Europe, and many believed Warsaw was a waypoint for these nightmarish places.

We did not want to be transferred to Warsaw, much less a concentration camp. Maybe Warsaw wasn't as bad as we had heard, but we didn't intend to find out. Once taken there, it would be impossible to escape from a ghetto surrounded by brick walls. We understood that if we were going to escape, we would have to do so now while we still could.

CHAPTER EIGHT

CUTTING LOOSE: ESCAPING THE GHETTO

W e had spent just over a year in the ghetto at Skierniewice when we began making plans for our escape. The great irony of our fear of Warsaw was that we had tried, and failed, to flee there only a year before. In a complete reversal of intent, we were now thinking of fleeing to *avoid* Warsaw.

Despite the famine and cold and mistreatment we faced in Skierniewice, the ghetto in Warsaw was worse for Jews. The Warsaw ghetto—which was far more secure, centralized, and dangerously crowded than the smaller ghettos—is perhaps the most photographed and filmed of all the Jewish ghettos, and it has appeared in numerous documentaries. The key differences between the Skierniewice and the Warsaw ghetto were that the latter was truly and totally closed, and escape was nearly impossible.

The impenetrable brick wall was designed to keep people in, but it was equally adept at keeping food and supplies out. People in the Warsaw ghetto died by the thousands for lack of food. In Skierniewice, our rations were what we were given, but we traded for more. There was also a legendary typhus epidemic in Warsaw so bad that news of it had reached us all the way in Skierniewice. Thousands succumbed to the disease. Medical care was scant to nonexistent.

We knew we would not make it in Warsaw for long, and we were terrified of being moved there. Most of our income came from my father and sister and Pinie being able to source materials to sell clothing. If they could not get leather and cloth, we would suffer severely. We also worried that my mother's packages would not make it through the walls, and we would lose that money too.

Lists of who were to be taken to the Warsaw ghetto were published around town. If your name appeared on such a list, you had to report at the time written next to your name. If not, they would come and arrest you. In this way, the Germans and Poles rounded up several thousand Jews at a time in various far-flung ghettos in towns and smaller cities in the countryside and transferred them to the ghetto in Warsaw. Hundreds of thousands of Jews were transported in this way—over three hundred thousand at least. From Warsaw, for many, the next stop would be Treblinka—a death camp nearly as big as Auschwitz. Some eight hundred thousand people perished in Treblinka over the next few years.

We did not know what Treblinka was at the time—in early 1941—and the death camps were not up and running just yet. But the Jews in Germany and occupied Poland understood that things were not good, that people were going missing en masse. Jews were being deported east, so we were told, but to where and to what end? We didn't know for sure what was happening, but we were beginning to suspect the worst. When people simply disappear in volume like that, you must expect the worst.

Given the conditions in the Warsaw ghetto, many did not even make it to the camps. One way or another, being deported to Warsaw generally meant that was the end—whether you died there or somewhere else was ultimately inconsequential.

This happened to people we knew. Jidel, the family friend who accompanied Pinie and me from the Polish camp at Posnan to my aunt and uncle's house in Skierniewice, died in this way. Jidel stayed behind in Skierniewice. When the Nazis came through and rounded everyone up, they took him to Warsaw. He either perished there or in Treblinka—it doesn't much matter, I suppose, exactly where he perished, only that he did. This happened to so many Jews all throughout Europe at this time. It is hard to get one's mind around the extent of it.

Do or Die

What all this meant to the Weiss family was this: escape was necessary, and the time was now. Warsaw was not an option. One day, our names were going to appear on one of the lists, and we would have to report to the train station, never to be heard from again. We had to come up with a plan to flee and go through with it, no matter how risky. To stay put, to risk deportation to Warsaw—that was the greatest risk of all.

My father and my uncle began planning our escape. I wasn't privy to the details, being only fourteen years old, but I knew what they were up to. They told me that my things should be ready to go so that when it was time, we could leave quickly.

I very much looked forward to leaving. The year in Skierniewice had been hard. And if Pinie and the rumors about the deplorable conditions in the Warsaw ghetto that were circulating were to be believed, there was no time to lose. I could hardly wait. I had my suitcase ready, just like my father instructed.

It was eventually decided that we would go to Tomaszów Mazowiecki, a small town near Lodz, which at that time did not have a ghetto. Tomaszów was where my father had been born. He had a sister there, the youngest of his siblings. She lived in the same wooden house that my father was born in and where his parents had raised him as a child. She lived there with her husband and their two daughters.

They chose this town not only because there was a family there with whom we could stay, but also because Tomaszów didn't have a ghetto yet—my father's sister had confirmed this fact, so we set about making plans to go there. After a year in Skierniewice, it was hard to imagine such a life! Traveling about town as one pleased, free to go where one wanted, no walls, no guards, no famine: a real life—it seemed almost impossible.

The plan was to break out of the ghetto by the cover of the night. The poorly built wall around the Skierniewice ghetto would be easy to penetrate. There were weak points in secluded areas through which we could break out with relative ease.

Of course, the Germans and Poles were aware that people sometimes escaped, but since most had nowhere to escape to, there were no mass exoduses, and the Germans did not much care. People fled routinely—three or four thousand people escaped Skierniewice as individuals and in small groups—but unless they left the country, there was nowhere Jews could go where they would not eventually end up in a ghetto. The walls were more about restricting movement around town than true incarceration.

We planned to use Germans' indifference to our advantage. We understood that our greatest risk was simply being seen by passersby. If we were seen trying to escape, German or Polish police might use it as an excuse to rob us or simply to torture us for their pleasure. This was a risk, but it was a manageable one. Yes, they might stop us if they saw us, but they would not be looking for us. We just had to do our best not to be conspicuous.

One night, my father woke my sister and me before dawn. It was still very dark out. "It's time," he said. "We're going now." He told us to grab our things, which we had already packed.

We met my uncle and aunt and their family outside, our bags in hand. He had his family with him and a horse-drawn carriage.

My uncle had run a taxi business in Skierniewice back before the ghetto was closed. He had owned a taxi car and several horse-drawn carriages. His customers were mostly Poles and Germans and some Jews, but once the fence went up around the ghetto, travel around and in the ghetto came to a halt, and so too did my uncle's profits. The ghetto couldn't support a taxi business when there was no one coming or going, and you could quickly walk from one end of the ghetto to the other in a matter of minutes. He had long since sold off the taxi car, horses, and the buggies for money to pay for food and other necessities. But he had kept one horse and a little wagon for personal use, and these we were to use to escape Skierniewice.

By cover of darkness, we loaded the carriage full of our belongings. We brought clothes, supplies, a little wood to burn, the sacks of potatoes from the basement, and what little we had that we could carry.

It was around five in the morning when we broke out of the ghetto. The sun was still not up. We found a secluded area where we could kick in the fence and rip the planks away to create a hole large enough to get the horse and buggy through the fence. The fence gave easily; no one really thought it would do otherwise. The enclosure around the ghetto was more of a psychological than physical barrier. Most people had nowhere to go and thus no reason to try to escape.

The riskiest proposition was passing by the German barracks, which we had to do to get out of Skierniewice. Here, I was indeed frightened of being stopped by German soldiers and arrested. There were military guards outside the barracks; they marched up and down the area in front. It was cold out, and we could see the clouds of their breaths and the snow shimmering on their boots in the moonlight.

We went around the back of the barracks in order not to disturb them. While I was sure they saw us, as we were not far away; we did not pass close enough by them for them to accost us without having to go out of their way to do so. Thankfully, they did not break formation. They could have, but they didn't. They continued their march in front of the barracks and paid us no mind. They didn't know who was passing by in the night, and they didn't seem to care. Maybe due to the cold, they didn't want to be bothered with stopping us. Their orders were to guard the barracks, not to look for escaping Jews. If we had gone to the front end of the barracks, they might have interfered, but we went around back to avoid them, and we were thus spared and allowed to leave Skierniewice unmolested.

On the Road

The road to Tomaszów was a hundred kilometers due north. It was already March by the time we broke out and fled, but it was still very cold. Polish winters are very cold, and this one was no exception.

There were eight of us in the caravan—my father, my sister and Pinie, my aunt, my uncle, his two children, and myself. My aunt's son was only two years younger than me and was good for conversation. The other child, the deaf-mute one, was from my uncle's first marriage. Unfortunately, we were not able to talk with him much as we did not know sign language, nor did he for that matter. He was very intelligent even though he could not communicate easily. He was very good with the horse, having helped to take care of his father's horses when he had the taxi business.

We had to walk so as not to tax the horse, which was already overburdened by all our possessions and the cart. The youngsters—meaning my cousin and me—were allowed to take turns sitting in the carriage for warmth or on the poor horse, but mostly we all walked like everyone else. In retrospect, I feel so bad for the horse. We're lucky he made it. Had he given out to exhaustion or the bitter cold, we would have had to abandon most of our things with the cart and walked to Tomaszów with only what we could carry. But as a child, you don't think about things that way. You think only that it is cold, that your legs are tired, that you have been walking all day from one bad place to another, and that you just want to sit down and rest.

We followed the main roads to Tomaszów because that was the only route we knew. This was risky for us as Jews because we were at the mercy of the people we passed on the road. Jews were not allowed to travel on the roads; to do so was an infraction punishable by death. Everything, it seemed, was now punishable by death if you were of Jewish descent. Taking the roads, taking the trains, leaving your house—even simply existing—was punishable by the death penalty.

Such laws were enforced randomly. The Germans had a lot on their plates and often would not respond unless the Poles drew their attention to someone. This happened often, unfortunately, and it happened to us on the way to Tomaszów. In Rawa, a town halfway to Tomaszów, we were stopped by a group of mean-spirited Poles. They recognized us as Jews and told us to stop where we were. They informed us that we were breaking the law by being out on the roads like this as if we did not know. These men made us wait by the side of the road while they reported us to the authorities.

We were very scared when the police arrived but were relieved to see that they were Polish officers, not Germans. Still, they were not so sympathetic. They demanded to know where we were traveling from and where to. Luckily, by a strange twist of fate, my uncle knew some of the officers and was able to talk to them. They looked our carriage over. They asked for documents.

My uncle brokered a deal with them. He not only knew these men but also knew how to deal with them—money. For a small bribe, they let us go without alerting the German authorities. It was very fortunate that my uncle knew these men as acquaintances—perhaps they took pity on us because of this. They could have simply stolen our money and everything we had and then alerted the German authorities.

If we hadn't had the money for a bribe or my uncle hadn't known them, I don't know what would have happened. Probably we would have all ended up in a concentration camp or prison somewhere, eventually a death camp. But we were lucky, and they allowed us to leave, which we did promptly.

We continued on our way. We were half frozen by now. It was still so cold outside, even in the middle of the day. Along the way, we met a kind, pious farmer, a Catholic man, who saw how cold we were and took pity on us. He could see that we were cold and, though not near death, truly miserable. He invited us into his house to have some hot tea he brewed over the stove while we warmed up inside. We sat for a while and talked with this man until we were warmer and a little less tired and able to set off again.

That farmer was kind, but he was of a rare type that does not take advantage of his fellow man. There were as many, if not more, like the Polish police who stopped us in Rawa. When we reached Tomaszów, another Polish man stopped us and again threatened to alert the Germans. We had to bribe this man too before we could enter the town. Some people showed us kindness, but many just tried to take advantage of our desperation. Hard times bring out the worst in some people.

Of course, hard times also bring out the best in many people. Desperate times call for heroic deeds. This farmer who had offered us shelter from the cold for a moment was not the first person to show my family and my kindness, nor would he be the last. It was through help and assistance like this that I made it through those years. We arrived in Tomaszów late that afternoon. We had passed through trial and tribulation, cold and extortion—but by the grace of God and the help of others, we had made it.

CHAPTER NINE

A GUN TO MY HEAD AND TYPHUS— MORE BRUSHES WITH DEATH

Upon arriving in Tomaszów, we made a beeline to my father's old house, where his sister's family now lived. We were met there by my two cousins, both girls and both older than me, in their twenties.

The older cousin met us at the door and welcomed us into their home. The house had two rooms, a living room, and a bedroom, and we stayed all in one room. It was intriguing to be in the house in which my father was born and where my grandparents had made their lives. There was so much family history under that roof.

It was good to see my aunt, whom I had not seen in years, and to get to know my two cousins better. It was wonderful to be around so much family. Tomaszów was a nice place to call home for a little while, and I enjoyed those first few weeks there.

The town itself was just another small town of about thirty thousand people. It was a manufacturing town back then, much like the larger city of Lodz nearby, and the entire economy of Tomaszów was built around textiles. There were whole industries for dyeing, manufacturing, and weaving. In better times, my father would have thrived there as a master tailor. But the economy suffered during the war, of course, and things were not so prosperous now, especially for Jews.

Here in Tomaszów, as in Skierniewice, it was a constant struggle for us to find food, but everyone managed to eat enough to survive. I could come and go from the Jewish district freely as I pleased, which allowed us to trade things with the Poles more easily than we had in Skierniewice. This was all thanks to Tomaszów not having a ghetto yet. *Yet*.

Of course, the good times were not to last. By the time summer came, the Nazis arrived and established a ghetto. They put planks up around the Jewish district like they had in Skierniewice.

My Big Mistake

Of course, once it became a ghetto, things got harder. But people managed to hold on and get by. By taking off my blue-and-yellow armband with the Star of David on it, I still managed to get in and out of the ghetto going through the fence as in Skierniewice. That star was intended to humiliate Jews. Instituted in 1939, it also made it easier to identify Jews for deportation to camps.

With the armband off, I could go to and from the Jewish area without being bothered, by passing as a German or Polish boy. No one here knew our family, so no one knew I was Jewish. I would often even go on long walks just for pleasure, sometimes around the ghetto and sometimes outside of it just like anybody else. I was lucky: many other Jews could not pass as Poles. I didn't look particularly Jewish; I had a German accent, and with no armband, no one was the wiser.

Taking the armband off was illegal, of course, but in my case, it was the safer thing to do. One time, while taking a letter to mail to my mother, I failed to remove my armband. I was stopped by some Germans who wanted to have some "fun" at my expense. They grabbed me and another boy off the street and took us into a courtyard area.

There were thirty or so people assembled there, boys from around town whom the Germans had snatched off the street also. They told us to lie down on the ground, which we did, and two German soldiers with bamboo canes began beating us for fun. I watched as they beat the other boy first. I watched and listened as they struck him with the cane for no reason at all. It was horrible to listen to him scream.

Then it was my turn. I refused to lie down for a beating. Several soldiers beat me, but I managed to free myself. I ran from the courtyard as fast as I could, but I didn't make it far. A German officer came up behind me with a gun drawn.

I stopped dead in my tracks.

He put the barrel to my head and cocked the hammer. *Click.*

"Do you want him back?" the German officer asked the soldiers who had been beating me.

"Yeah, yeah," they said. "We want him back."

The soldiers grabbed me and took me back to the courtyard where they beat me harder. It was serendipitous that they weren't done with me just yet. Otherwise, the German soldier with the gun would probably have shot me in the head then and there on the street. He had only to pull the trigger, and I would have been dead. I didn't even know at the time quite how close I had come. I didn't understand then how guns worked or what the sound of the hammer clicking was. I only realized it later when my friends explained to me how you cock a gun before pulling the trigger. At the time, I had had no idea that the gun was ready to fire, how easy it would have been for him to pull the trigger and how close I had come to being murdered in the street.

Eventually, the German soldiers tired of us and they let us go. There were Jewish police standing on the corner. They spotted us limping away from the courtyard and came over to investigate. Some of the boys had blacked out there in the street. I collapsed, though I didn't black out. I was just nauseated and sick and wanted them to take me with them to the police station. They did.

Back at the station, one of the Jewish policemen cleaned me up with a bit of rubbing alcohol and bandaged my wounds. I was covered in bruises from head to toe. They then took me to the Jewish hospital in Tomaszów to be checked out. The doctors said I had no internal injuries and that I would be okay. But I was swollen everywhere. Every last part of my body hurt and throbbed. The hospital decided to keep me overnight for observation to make sure I was okay.

The next day, a German officer came to the hospital. He said I could not leave the hospital, or I would be arrested because I had fought with another boy. This was a lie, of course, but I couldn't object. I couldn't tell the doctors what had really happened, which surely, they already knew because of the German having been there. I would have been punished for telling them the truth. I would have been in even more danger and possibly endangered my family too. Instead, I just lied and said, "Yes, I had fought with a boy." Once I said this, the German left me alone, and the hospital released me later that day.

I returned to my aunt's house. My father saw me all swollen and bruised and was very angry, but also sad. We were all desperate. Between the beating I had taken and the fact that Tomaszów had turned into a closed ghetto, we knew that we would have to leave there soon too.

The constant moving was stressful. It was as if we were on a constant treadmill, trying to stay one step ahead of the Nazis. Every time we came to a new place, we thought we could survive. And we could have if they would have left us alone. But the Nazis wouldn't. Everywhere we went, they came and pushed us into ghettos.

By this time, Rosa and Pinie had already left Tomaszów. They had found another place in Zakrzówek, which was a small town near the city of Lublin that did not have a ghetto yet. They had left as soon as they put up the wall around the ghetto. My father and I, as well as my uncle and aunt, had not gone because we knew Zakrzówek would be just like Tomaszów: that it had no ghetto was no guarantee that it would not have one soon.

I did end up going to Zakrzówek, though. Tomaszów had become too dangerous for me. The Nazis began regularly rounding up Jewish men and boys over fourteen years of age as they had done to me. But not everyone was as lucky to be let go as I had been the last time. The Nazis would come and find Jews on the streets and in our houses and take us away, sometimes for beatings and executions, but other times to be transported to concentration camps. These mass seizures of Jewish men were called *razzias*. To avoid them, I had to go into hiding whenever I heard that it was happening.

Protected by Typhus

We would do anything not to be taken away. When I caught word of one currently underway in Tomaszów, I hid in a building where I knew there was a typhus epidemic in hopes that the Nazis would not look for me there. One occupant of this building was already in hospital with typhus, others were sick, but I had no choice. I hid there, hoping the Nazis would not come in after me. They didn't, but I fell sick with abdominal typhus. It took me weeks to recover.

My sister wrote me a letter, asking, "Why don't you come here? Come to Zakrzówek." She believed I would be safer there where there was no ghetto. After my beating, the regular *razzias,* and a severe bout of abdominal typhus, I couldn't help but agree. And so, I did go to stay with her. She made it sound nice and safe there, and I had little interest in staying in Tomaszów and being subjected to more beatings and illness.

In July 1941, I left Tomaszów and headed to Zakrzówek by train to join my sister. Traveling by train was forbidden for Jews and was punishable by death. Despite this risk, it was easy for me to acquire a train ticket and travel between cities by myself. I was not recognized as a Jew. The Germans assumed that I was a Pole, and the Poles assumed I was German. I spoke Polish and so I ordered my ticket in Polish, and when we stopped in Dresden on the way, I ordered my ticket in German. The German inspectors did not stop me. They were oblivious to my true identity.

I was also very fortunate to have a birth certificate that said, "No Religion" on it rather than "Jewish." How that happened, I do not know. My sister's passport denoted her as a Jew, but mine did not. This was a great aid in getting around Germany and occupied Poland undetected. With my passport, my nondescript looks, my German accent, and my Jewish armband hidden away in my suitcase, I was able to travel freely and without fear.

It was July when I arrived in Zakrzówek. Fourteen days after falling sick with typhus in Tomaszów, I again fell sick of it in Zakrzówek. I must have brought the disease with me, not having fully recovered. I was seriously ill again, and this time, I became delirious from fever. I didn't know what was going on. Pinie took me to a Jewish hospital in Krasnik. The hospital was very primitive, lacked resources, and was seriously overcapacity due to the outbreaks of typhus and other epidemics. There were two patients on each bed. There was not enough medicine and food. The equipment was old and dated. But the care we got from the doctors and nurses was very good, and while many died, most survived, especially the young. I had the will to survive. I struggled to do so, but I struggled hard and eventually pulled through again and got better.

I thank the Jewish hospital in Zakrzówek for my survival. If I had stayed in Tomaszów and had fallen sick again, so much more violently this time, I may not have pulled through. There would have been no one there to care for me except for my father. More luck or divine providence? I do not know what had protected me so far, but I was grateful to the universe.

A New Home, for Now

Like Tomaszów, Zakrzówek was not so bad a place to be in the first days after arriving. It was a very small town of three thousand residents, not far from Lublin. There was one particularity to the geographical layout of Zakrzówek that made it attractive to my sister and Pinie. Zakrzówek was a small town only about five kilometers long that was spread out around one main road. There was a small town-center at its heart, with a few different stores and shops, including a toy store. This town-center was also the Jewish area, which is why there was no ghetto there. There was only one main road going in and out of town with the ghetto right in the center. This meant that the site of any potential ghetto would be a chokepoint that divided the town in half, cutting off the main thoroughfare.

We were almost sure that there would be no ghetto there. If there were to be a ghetto, it would have to remain at least partially open to allow traffic through town. Because of this, Jews were free to travel around town as they pleased, making Zakrzówek seem to be the ideal place to wait out the troubles.

After a month of being in Zakrzówek, my sister and I decided that it would be best to send for my father and bring him here too. Zakrzówek was still safe, and Tomaszów had gotten dangerous. I was to go back to Tomaszów and bring my father with me. It made the most sense for me to go, despite my young age, because I was so good at traveling undetected as a Jew. All I had to do was speak in German and not wear my armband, and no one suspected a thing.

I went back to Tomaszów then to get my father, and we traveled together back to Zakrzówek. On the way back, we stopped at the station in Krasnik, which is right next door to Zakrzówek.

At one of the train stops along the way to Lublin, we had to get off the train and connect to the next train by taking sleighs. We traveled seven kilometers by sleigh with a group of Poles. Along the way, we were stopped by a German officer who was collecting taxes from the Polish farmers in the countryside. He was traveling with Polish officers as well. One of the Polish officers stopped everyone to ask who we were and where we were coming from. We were scared that we would be recognized as Jewish, but they let us pass through with all the Poles.

Afterward, the Poles we were traveling with told us that we were lucky that the Germans and Poles that had stopped us had not recognized us as Jews. We had thought we were fooling them, but they had known our identities from the start! The Poles we were traveling with took a great risk in not betraying us. Had we been discovered, the officers might have shot all six of them too along with us. It was very benevolent of them to have assumed such risk on our behalf.

From there, we boarded a train back to Lublin and headed back into the Jewish area in the heart of town where we were, for the time being, safe at my sister's house. We had made the trip successfully. Everyone hugged when they were reunited.

Unfortunately, we had been able to carry very little with us, and my father had to leave behind all his sewing equipment. There was no way we could carry all his machines on the train. This meant that it was harder for him to make money because he didn't have the proper equipment. My father could no longer work and make clothes.

We still did okay though because he had brought with him several suits he had made previously and packed them into a suitcase to bring along. He sold these off slowly and any other valuables, one at a time, to buy food and other necessities. To make the money last, he had to sell them sparingly and use the money sparingly, but we stretched it as much as we could. We also got money from my mother's packages still, which we relied upon more and more. Remarkably, they were still coming through.

Back in the Ghetto

Before too long, the Jewish district in Zakrzówek was made into a ghetto as well. They put up planks around the Jewish area and then diverted traffic around it. After this, things got worse for everyone. Food was very tight for those who didn't have money, and few did have money. Most people barely scraped by. You had to have some means to feed yourself—something to trade, money coming in from the outside, things to smuggle.

We were a little worse off for not having my father's machinery for making clothes, but we still did okay with what we had. It was bearable when you had money or a way to make money, but most didn't have much of either, and they suffered terribly for it. Most were looking for money as ravenously as they were always looking for food: they were the same thing in the ghetto. When food, shelter, and necessities are scarce, you realize how precious they are and how money is merely a means to an end.

Once the ghetto was established, my ability to get around town undetected as a Jew became very important to our survival. I wasn't given this freedom -- I took it. I had no special rights. Only what I took. And I was learning to take as much as I could. I began smuggling goods in and out of the ghetto.

My father couldn't move about the ghetto as I could. I had an exceptional level of freedom because I spoke German and had a passport and didn't look Jewish. Without my armband, I was the same as the rest of the Poles. No one suspected who I was. They didn't ask me, and I didn't volunteer information. If someone did ask prying questions, I pretended not to understand. I played the part of a dumb, clueless teenager.

Smuggling was a good way to make cash to help feed my family, but it was not without its risks. I once brought some flour to the train station packed away as baggage. The Polish train conductors stopped me and demanded that I open the bag for inspection.

"I can't. It's locked," I said, which was true, though I had the key on me.

"Well, unlock it, boy!" one of the conductors demanded.

"I can't," I said. "I lost the key."

They demanded to know what was in the bag. I told them it was nothing but my mother's dirty laundry. I had simply lost the key and couldn't open it! I had nothing to hide, I insisted. I just wanted to get my mother's laundry back to her.

The conductors looked upon this story suspiciously. I was afraid they would break the case open and I would be exposed. They held me at the station for the German police. Thankfully, speaking German, I was able to convince a German policeman that it was all one big misunderstanding. He believed my story about the dirty laundry, and he told the Poles to release the doors and allow me to leave. I thanked the German officer profusely. I was lucky to have duped him. If he had known the truth! If I hadn't spoken German with a German accent, I never would have gotten away with it.

When I got back to Rosa's house, she and Pinie demanded to know where I had been all day. I told them what had happened. Pinie looked at me sternly and said, "No more, no more! No more smuggling." And that was the end of my smuggling days.

All in all, life in Zakrzówek wasn't good, but it was bearable. On a typical day, I would meet up with friends or spend time with family. I also worked, selling clothing. There were no Jewish schools here, unfortunately; none of the ghettos had real schools. Sometimes volunteer teachers would pitch in and teach the young children basic lessons, but older kids like myself did not get schooled. Perhaps you, reader, hated school in your youth, hated it so much you played truant or feigned sickness to escape the drudgery to study. Or, if you didn't "hate" it, perhaps you remember being happy on snow days or on the last day of the semester when the promise of the long summer recess of doing exactly as you please swelled your heart with joy and freedom as you walked out of the school gates. I understand that school is a chore for most young people, but I would have gladly been cooped up all day every day in a schoolroom with teachers barking at me about my homework because knowledge is freedom and knowledge is power, even if the classroom feels oppressive. So do not feel any envy that my youth was not spent hunkered over textbooks; pity me.

As the years wore on, I fell seriously behind in my studies, and I worried that I would never catch up. This would end up being true—I would never go back to school again. My life was completely and utterly derailed. You never recover from such a thing—not fully.

CHAPTER TEN

1942—OUR BLEAKEST YEAR YET

A ll this traveling from ghetto to ghetto was tedious and trying, but it was worth it and necessary: it was the reason I survived the Holocaust. The only other option was to stay put and let the Nazis shepherd us where they wanted. Had we stayed put, I have no doubt that I would have ended up in Warsaw and eventually a concentration camp or death camp. I would have ended up going up a smokestack somewhere, like so many others.

The years 1941 to 1942 were a low point for Europe at large, and the Jews suffered particularly hard. We had initially thought the war would be over quickly. We thought England, France, and the United States would step in and stop the Nazis. But the US had not entered the war right away due to staunch isolationism that World War I had instilled in the American citizenry. Still, we had thought that England and France would swoop in and win the war quickly. This did not happen. France had been invaded in May 1940 and fallen officially by the next month. It had been divided up into separate areas under Axis control. France would remain under Axis control until liberated late in the summer of 1944 following the Allied landings on D-Day.

After the fall of France, English forces fell back and withdrew from the mainland. England did not fall, but it endured years of air raids and bombings that kept Allied forces at bay. Back on the mainland, any hope of liberation had been dashed.

The worst year, the year that dashed our hopes most of all, was 1942. The German war against the Russians had begun in 1941. By 1942, a second push resulted in more gains. This forced Germany into a war of attrition against the largest country on earth. That massive endeavor would stretch the Nazi forces too thin and eventually result in the downfall of the Third Reich, but at the time, Germany appeared to be making progress, and the outlook for Europe looked very grim. German forces couldn't take Moscow, and they faced an infamous and sound defeat at the Battle of Leningrad. But from continental Europe, the tone in 1942 was one of hopelessness. Europe, from the Volga to the Atlantic, was in Hitler's hands.

The war had been raging since 1939, but President Roosevelt had refused to enter the war immediately. The papers pleaded our case in Europe. They wrote "America! America!" pleading with Roosevelt as if the United States was Europe's only hope, and perhaps it was. The United States did enter the war, of course, but not until December 1941. The Americans had to practically be dragged into the war. Only after the surprise attack on Pearl Harbor did the United States declare war on Japan. Germany then declared war on the United States as part of a defense agreement—only then did the United States declare war on Germany. But their arrival in Europe would not be immediate.

The Americans came to the war late, and they did not enter the Western Front while they were ramping up military production in the United States. The Americans coordinated bombing campaigns with the British, but it was not until D-Day in June 1944 that Allied troops landed in continental Europe in full force.

In 1942, before the war began to turn against the Axis Powers, things looked bleak in Europe. The Nazis had defeated France. Great Britain was still reeling from the blitzkrieg that had ravaged the nation for two years. Hitler's hordes were able to advance further into Russia with the best-armed, most-advanced army the world had yet seen. They had pushed the Russians back and were almost all the way to Stalingrad. And in Poland, the Final Solution was now well underway.

Rumors of Mass Murder

Jews were being taken from the Jewish ghettos of Poland and Germany in great numbers for extermination at newly constructed death camps. A couple of months after we had left Skierniewice, the Nazis came into the ghetto and transferred all the Jews to Warsaw, just as we had feared. (This is when Jidel, our family friend, was taken as well.) They did not arrest everyone—they didn't have to. They made a terrible and gruesome display. German soldiers randomly selected several dozen people wearing the Jewish armband—including men, women, and children—and executed them publicly. They shot them in the street and then announced that this was what would become of anyone who failed to report at the train station for transfer to Warsaw. I did not know this at the time, of course, for we had already fled from Skierniewice to Tomaszów.

In the following days, some fled Skierniewice as we had, but most people reported to the train station as demanded, either for fear of being murdered or because they had nowhere else to go. All across Europe, the ghettos were being emptied and consolidated in this way.

Our family, partly by design and partly by stroke of luck, managed to stay one step ahead of this process by leaving ghettos as they were closed off. We moved from Skierniewice to Tomaszów to Zakrzówek to avoid being brought to an encampment. We worked very hard to make this happen, but we also were simply lucky not to have been captured and taken to Warsaw at any point along the way. Extremely lucky, to be honest.

Concentration camps used for incarceration and forced labor had been in existence in Germany since as early as the mid-1930s. But "death camps" were a newer phenomenon that began popping up all around Germany and occupied Poland. As early as October 1941, the German SS officers received orders to begin building camps solely for the extermination of Jews and others "not fit for life" under the Nazi doctrine of the "Final Solution." We know now that that included gay people, Gypsies, disabled people, intellectuals, dissidents, and communists.

The first death camp, Chelmno, was ready and operational by

December 1941. By mid-1942, death camps were also in operation at Belzec, Sobibor, Treblinka, Auschwitz, and elsewhere. Jews were not detained long at these camps. They were brought in by train and tricked into entering gas chambers under the pretense that they were showers. Their bodies were then incinerated or dumped into mass graves.

We didn't understand the extent of the atrocities at the time, of course. We knew only that atrocities were happening, but we had no way of knowing the true mind-boggling scope of what Hitler and the Nazis had set in motion. We couldn't have imagined that they really meant to kill all Jews. We knew they were killing Jews, but the notion that they would try to kill all of us never occurred to us: it was beyond imagination. We heard rumors, but we thought it impossible. We thought, how could they possibly shoot us all? Surely, they cannot. It would be madness! But this was before the mechanized, industrialized gas chambers that were being used for this purpose had come to light. We had heard tell of Jews being mass murdered deep in Russia, but we hadn't imagined anything like the pictures that surfaced after the death camps were liberated.

These sites "processed" millions of Jews in a few short years in what represented the deadliest phase of the Holocaust—the years between 1942 and 1944. In many parts of Poland and Germany, over 90 percent of the Jewish population was exterminated in this way. Six million Jews were murdered, two-thirds of all those living in Europe at the time. Eleven million people in all were put to death for no good reason. There can be no good reason for such a thing.

This could have been my fate as well, but it was not. Ironically, I was spared by escaping back into Germany in 1942, shortly before this campaign of terror kicked into high gear. I was spared, yet again, by being willing to keep moving coupled with a healthy dose of serendipity.

CHAPTER ELEVEN

SAVED BY A SEWING MACHINE—ESCAPE TO GERMANY AS FORCED LABOR

All these problems in the Polish ghettos were taking place while my mother was still in Barsinghausen, Germany, living in one small room in the attic of our old family home. She was working long hours for a small sewing business owned by the Schmak company during the day and nights and weekends for Mr. Brandt, the man who bought our house for practically nothing, thanks to Germany's campaign against Jewish property owners. The money that she made working these two jobs is what made sure that our far-flung family had something to eat and wear no matter what ghetto we found ourselves in.

In 1942, the Schmak company was planning a major expansion that included the opening of a new factory dedicated to manufacturing uniforms for the German military. My mother's employer mentioned in passing that they were struggling to find enough high-quality modern sewing machinery for the new garment factory. Up until this point, my mother had been working on large old-fashioned looms, hand-operated spinning wheels, and other outdated machines. In order to mass-produce military uniforms, the Schmak company needed modern machines— and lots of them. These machines were expensive and difficult to source in Europe's devastated wartime economy where even the most basic necessities were scarce.

As luck would have it though, my father had purchased a modern Pfaff sewing machine back when we were all together in Barsinghausen. He had bought the machine in the late 1930s with the intention of going to America. When he had applied for a visa before the war even started, he showed the immigration office his receipt for the machine with which he planned to launch a tailoring business in the United States. (Unfortunately, the immigration office informed us that there was an eleven-year wait for German Jews seeking to come to America at that time—we were not the only Jewish family trying to flee Germany in the 1930s.)

When the immigration office denied our application for visas, the machine had seemed like something of an unnecessary, frivolous purchase since we could not actually leave Germany. It was a fine machine, but more than my father needed for a small one-man tailoring business. As it happened, though, this machine would end up saving my very life.

My mother told Mr. Schmak about the Pfaff sewing machine. He was delighted to hear the news of this machine, which was exactly the kind he needed for the new factory. Being a smart, resourceful woman, my mother brokered a deal with him: she would give him the sewing machine, but only if her children were its operators. If he would write a letter to the employment office in Poland asking for foreign worker visas for her children to come back to Germany to work at the Schmak company, then the Pfaff sewing machine was his, free of charge (fig. 7). My mother insisted that I would be an asset to the company. I had learned to operate the Pfaff myself while working at my father's tailoring business.

Figure 7

Mr. Schmak agreed to my mother's deal and wrote a letter to the employment office on my behalf. My mother had wanted to send for both Rosa and me, but Rosa did not want to leave Pinie behind. She refused to abandon her husband in the ghetto. Since Rosa would not go, I was to go alone. This was a more practical arrangement because I had a passport that did not denote me as Jewish. My sister's passport said she was Jewish, which would make it difficult for her to get approval from the employment bureaus in Poland and Germany. In retrospect though, I wish she had tried to make it out of Poland too because, as it would later turn out, she never would.

Strangers to the Rescue

Acquiring a foreign worker visa was no easy task—especially for a Jewish boy. The only reason that my application was approved was because Mr. Schmak had a friend in the Hanover Employment Office by the name of Mr. Blumenfeld, a kind German man, whom he knew well. Mr. Schmak wrote Mr. Blumenfeld a letter requesting that I be allowed to come to Germany to work in the new garment factory as a foreign worker. The letter asked for me specifically by name and claimed that as a skilled tailor, I was needed urgently for "very essential work in the defense industry." Mr. Schmak reminded him that because the new factory was to produce uniforms for the German military, this was an urgent matter of national security and an important and urgent part of the war effort.

Mr. Blumenfeld in turn wrote a letter on my behalf to the employment office in Lublin. A few weeks passed, and I received a letter from the employment office in Lublin telling me that my application for a foreign worker visa had been approved. I was informed that I would be allowed to leave Poland and travel to Germany. After three and a half years in Polish ghettos, I was going home to live with my mother in Germany. My father said he would miss me, but he wanted me to be safe. I would be safer with my mother in Germany than I was with him in Poland, hopping from one dangerous ghetto after another.

What irony that I would escape *to* Germany! But that is exactly what happened. Technically, I was being returned from Poland to Germany as a forced laborer; and once the letters were sent, I had no choice about whether to go or not. In practice, however, my mother had tricked the Nazi state into sending me from the ghetto back into her care and the safety of Mr. Brandt's house: such a small victory felt immense.

There is no way to overstate how lucky I was that this happened. I have heard of no other cases of Jews escaping the ghettos in this way. It is possible, of course, but it was exceedingly difficult and rare. That this worked was nothing short of miraculous. Were it not for Mr. Schmak and Mr. Blumenfeld, my application would never have been approved, and you must realize that I did not even know these men. Mr. Schmak only wrote the letter because he wanted the sewing machine. I do not know why Mr. Blumenfeld cooperated. His surname has Jewish origins, so perhaps that is why he took pity on me. I never met him, so I do not know, but I am eternally grateful for his help in getting my work permit.

Despite all the people who played a role in my escape, I thank my mother above all for helping me escape the ghettos in Poland. I owe my long life to her shrewd and cunning maneuvers that saved me from places where I had already come close to death from disease and malnutrition. I had fallen sick with typhus multiple times, and I was in very ill health.

I almost didn't make it out of Poland when I again fell seriously ill before departing for Germany. This time it was pneumonia, but no one knew what was wrong with me at first. The only doctor around who would treat Jews was Dr. Foerster, an exile from Vienna. He himself was sick at the time and unable to treat me or anyone else. The Jewish Council in Zakrzówek had begged the German commanders to send another doctor to the area. These requests had fallen on deaf ears for a long time, and we had gone without a doctor.

I was too ill to travel. I was afraid I would miss my chance to go to Germany. Finally, though, in May, we got a new doctor in Zakrzówek. This doctor was also in terrible health too and nearly famished himself. He looked as bad as his worst patients. He had come from a terrible concentration camp very nearby, which we had only heard rumors about until then that predominantly held Jews from Vienna. This doctor had no medical instruments or medicines with him. He examined me by tapping my chest with his fingers and putting his ear against my chest to listen to my breathing. The diagnosis was "scattered pneumonia."

We were grateful to have a doctor again, any doctor, and our hearts commanded us to help this man, a Jew suffering only on account of his religion and ethnicity. But he was more affected by the ill conditions of the ghetto than many of the patients whom he served, and it was already too late for him when he arrived in Zakrzówek. He died shortly after arriving and diagnosing me—he had helped me but help for him had come too late. I managed to pull through, thanks to this good man.

This poor doctor had written me a prescription for penicillin after diagnosing my pneumonia. I managed to receive medicine from a Polish pharmacy, the only one in town, probably since the Germans needed me as a foreign worker. My father, my sister, and Pinie nursed me back to health, making sure I always had good food to eat. Thanks to the medicine and the care of my family, I again recovered quickly from my fourth bout of major illness in Poland in as many years. I had gotten jaundice in Zbaszyn, abdominal typhus in Tomaszów, and then epidemic typhus in Zakrzówek. Now I could add pneumonia to the list.

Although I was still weak, I was now well enough to travel to Germany, just in time to report to the employment office in Lublin for my scheduled departure.

When I showed up at the employment office, there were several hundred other men there also awaiting transport to Germany as foreign workers, most of them Polish volunteer workers. There was a small celebration thrown in our honor. Polish volunteers handed out food to me and the other foreign workers. We were given vegetables, hot soup, and other delicious foods that I had rarely had in the last few years living in the ghettos. It is indescribable what good vegetable soup tastes like after subsisting on a diet of potato soup for several years. They played music over the loudspeakers, and some people danced. It was a good time.

We were photographed laughing together in front of the employment office for the local paper. The caption under the photo would read something like "Volunteer Poles go to work in Germany." I was the only Jew among them, unbeknownst to all. The Poles believed I was of German ethnicity due to my German accent.

From the employment office, we were taken to the train station in Lublin for transport to Germany. My fare, RM52.70, was billed to the Schmak company. I was only sixteen years old at this time but feeling quite independent and firmly within the realm of adulthood after all that I had lived through and seen. I was already accustomed to traveling alone on the train after having traveled by train to my sister in Zakrzówek and then back to Tomaszów to fetch my father and back again.

Fully fed for the journey, we boarded the train. It was not a regular passenger train with regular passengers. It was a transport train. All the passengers were Polish volunteers and forced laborers like me. We were transported while watched by guards. This first leg of the trip felt very militarized and bureaucratic.

The trip was a two-day ride to Dresden. We slept upright in our seats the first night, and when we woke in the morning, we could tell we had already crossed the border into Germany. We could tell simply by looking at the scenery out the window that flew by as we passed from station to station. Instead of the unpaved streets of Poland, we now saw tarmac roads. The houses had real roofs instead of straw ones. The most marked difference was how much less devastated the interior of Germany was in comparison to Poland. There was far less destruction from bombing and warfare in Germany at this point in the war.

On the second day, we arrived at the Dresden station where we disembarked. The soldiers took us to a facility holding center to be examined by doctors. The men and women were separated into two groups and taken to different rooms. We were told to undress completely so that we could be deloused before being released into Dresden. Our clothes were to be taken from us so that they could be boiled, washed, and dried.

I removed my clothes hesitantly because I did not want my circumcision to give away the fact that I was Jewish. Few people in Europe practiced circumcision except for Jews, and it was a dead giveaway. Feigning bashfulness, I held my hands over my genitals. I did not want the Germans to see, but I did not want the Poles to see either. Many of the latter seemed very nice, but there was no way to know which among them would cry out, "Jew! Jew! Jew!" This was the only word that some of them could say in German—they had learned it to expose people in situations like this, either for personal gain or just out of pure meanness.

After they took our clothes, the Germans ushered us into a big room where we were to bathe. They led men twenty at a time into the showers. My heart rate quickened when I saw the showers. I was familiar with the Nazi practice of shipping people by train to extermination camps with fake showers. The victims would stand naked, waiting for the faucets to come on—but when the faucets did come on, it was not water that spewed forth, but carbon monoxide or Zyklon B, a cyanide gas. Millions died this way.

All this was going through my mind, causing my hands to shake and my back to sweat. But what could I do? Nothing. When it was my turn, I was taken with twenty others into the showers. The faucets were connected to overhead sprinkler systems. The floor was wet, which was at least a little reassuring.

A German man came around with a bucket of foul-smelling soft soap. He used a ladle to slap globs of this soap onto our backs and into our hands. Again, I wondered—was this poison? Was the wet floor a ploy to disguise the fact that the sprinklers would release an asphyxiating gas? These worries were hardly unfounded. We were nothing but Poles and Jews. We were nothing to the Nazis.

In the end, everything was as it seemed. The water that came from the sprinklers was only water. The foul-smelling soap was actual soap with a pesticide added for delousing purposes. We bathed quickly and were handed towels to dry off before being sent to the next room where we lined up one after the other, awaiting inspection by the doctors.

Here again I was afraid that my circumcision would be the death of me. I was carrying a letter of protection with me that clearly stated that though I was half-Jewish, I was urgently needed in Barsinghausen for work in the defense industry. Still, letter or not, I was afraid of the German doctor. There was no way to be sure that a simple letter would protect me. People disappeared all the time in Nazi Germany. My safety was not guaranteed.

My hands were still covering my genitals when I reached the front of the line.

"Hands out and turn around," the doctor ordered.

I had no choice but to comply. I pulled my hands away. I was completely exposed before the doctor. My circumcision must have been obvious. I waited for the inevitable gasp and for him to call in the guards, for him to shout out that I was a Jew—that there was a Jew on the premises. But the doctor studied my genitals for a moment. He glanced up at my face and then away. "Next!" he said.

I again covered myself with my hands and continued past the doctor to the line at the other end of the room. The German doctor was there to detect sexually transmitted diseases, not Jews, but I was still certain that he would expose me. I stood in line for my clothes and then quickly dressed, marveling at the fact that I had made it through the medical inspection. Had he taken mercy on me, or was there some guardian angel watching over me, blinding this man to my circumcision? Either way, I had made it past this major hurdle.

We received our deloused clothing back. It had been washed and boiled as promised and was cleaner than my clothes had been in a long time. As harrowing as the process had been, it felt good to step out onto the streets of Dresden in clean, fresh clothing.

From the station, I reported to the employment office in Dresden. There was a friendly official there who took my letter of protection and other documents. After reading them over, he issued me a special ticket so that I could ride the regular train to Hanover, the closest station to Barsinghausen. He even accompanied me back to the train to make sure I boarded the correct train. We talked along the way, and he bade me good fortune on my travels.

The Final Leg toward Home

I was now free to travel alone, but I stayed with some of the Polish volunteers who were also headed to Hanover. This train was just a normal passenger train to Hanover. There were no German guards, except the ones that normally patrolled the trains. I sat in third class with other Germans, and it was as if I were just anyone else. No one questioned me about who I was or if I was Jewish. No one threatened me. It was an amazing experience after so many years of persecution. No one knew who I was or that I was Jewish. I was not forced to wear the Jewish armband stuffed deep down into my luggage. It was a novel experience now to be treated the same as everyone else—as a normal human being.

This was all a charade, of course. I was Jewish (and proudly so). If the Germans or the Poles had known this, I might have been stopped regardless of my letter of protection and work permit. I might have been either shot on the spot or sent back to Poland and ended up in a smokestack. But I was no longer so scared of these possibilities. By now, I had become accustomed to traveling in secrecy. So many times before, I had simply removed my armband with the Star of David, carried my birth certificate and papers that said "No Religion," and emphasized my own German accent when I spoke. In this way, I traveled all across Europe without the fear most Jews experienced in Nazi Germany in 1942. Now was no different. If anything, it was better: I was traveling legally and had the documents to prove it.

Our train arrived in Hanover the following day. Immediately upon deboarding, I started the long walk to Barsinghausen, a hike I had done so many times as a boy. As of 1942, the war had not quite come to this part of Europe in full force. The front was far away, and Hanover had not been bombed heavily since the English forces had fallen back off the continent over a year ago.

When I arrived in Barsinghausen later that day, I returned to my old house where I was greeted by my mother whom I had not seen in three years. My family was shocked to see me. My mother and her sisters couldn't believe their eyes even though they had known I was coming. My relatives and acquaintances didn't know what to do with me upon arrival. I looked horrible, they said, and they threw their arms around me.

I spent the first night back at my old house that I had not slept in for so long, and while it was now technically Mr. Brandt's house, it was still so good to be home among so many friends and so much family. I owe all this to my mother and my father's Pfaff sewing machine, which is still on display today at my son's home in Baltimore.

CHAPTER TWELVE

REUNITED WITH MY MOTHER—
BACK IN BARSINGHAUSEN

Mr. Brandt allowed me to take up residence in the house with my mother under the condition that she continued to make wreaths for him. I often saw my mother staying up late into the night weaving wreaths. She never took days off, not even on weekends. Her fingertips were permanently chapped and bleeding. This she did for her family so that I could stay on at the house—so that she could spend the few earned marks on things to send to my sister, Rosa, and her husband, my father, and the rest of our family who were still trying to survive in the Zakrzówek ghetto until the war was over. My mother was an amazing woman.

I didn't have to share a room with her, which was good, as I would not have wanted to crowd her. She deserved her space and rest at the end of a long day (and night). Luckily, there was a second room on the third floor, a small adjoining room, in which I slept. It was practically a closet, really; but after sleeping with several, often dozens, in a room, it was nice and even a little strange to now have even a modicum of privacy.

While my mother had been spared the horror and hardships of the ghettos, she had faced her own troubles here in Germany. The Gestapo, upon unearthing her marriage to my father and her conversion to Judaism, had begun requiring her to report to the police regularly as "a Polish Jew" even though she had not been born Jewish. She very easily could have been arrested by the Gestapo, though so far they had left her alone. She was permitted to continue working in the clothing factory, which kept her out of the ghettos, and in that way she had been lucky. And we too had been lucky, of course, because her job allowed her to send money to us in the ghetto.

Now I too had the power to help my family in the same way. My work permit didn't just allow me to work at the Schmak company—it was required that I do so. This is what it meant to be a foreign laborer. I was basically a slave, an indentured servant. I did not complain though, nor did I feel the compulsion to; I was happy to have escaped the precariousness of Poland. I started working at the garment factory almost immediately.

My health was not good those first few months. While the Polish ghettos had not killed me, they had sapped my strength. I was half-starved and very weak, still sickly from the lingering effects of pneumonia. You could see my ribs in fine detail. My overall health was so poor that I had trouble standing for the entirety of my work shifts and often had to take breaks to lie down. At times, I was barely able to work in those first few months. Still, I went to work. I had to. My life depended on it—if I didn't go to work, I would lose my work permit and could be sent back to Poland.

Mr. Schmak and his wife, both of whom worked in the factory office, were humane employers. They gave me only easy tasks those first few months while I rebuilt my strength. They expected me to show up, but they did nothing to alleviate my poor condition. Suffering through my days, I came home at nights to collapse into bed. Night sweats from weakness kept me from sleeping well.

My mother cared for me during those first few months and worked hard to find extra food for me. You needed a ration card in order to buy food during the war. The authorities strictly controlled how much people consumed to ensure there was enough food and other basic supplies for the German soldiers and so that the stores would not run out.

Upon first arriving, I did not have a ration card and so couldn't get food from the breadlines and stores. We were scared to go to the Barsinghausen municipality to request my own food rations. They would have asked all kinds of questions about my background and if I was Jewish. I still had my letter of protection and my work permit, but we worried about going before the German authorities. There would have been Gestapo there.

So instead of getting my own ration card, we lived off just my mother's rations those first months. She gave me almost everything that we were both entitled to, often going hungry herself so that I could eat and regain my strength. Sometimes people at work would give me their extra sandwiches at my mother's request. Slowly, I built my strength back and put a little weight back on.

Eventually, it was clear I was going to need my own rations. There was no other way but to apply for them at the municipal office. My mother accompanied me to the Barsinghausen municipality to register. Unfortunately, one of the officials working there was "SH," the cruel man who had detained our family way back in October 1938 when the Jewish pogroms had first begun. He recognized us and made it his job to make the process very difficult.

We had to answer many questions about my nationality and religion. They didn't want to give me ration cards for food and clothing even though my foreign worker papers should have entitled me to these basic necessities.

My mother was persistent though and would not be deterred. "He needs these," she demanded. "He is German. He is here with a work permit."

The difficulty was in deciding how to register me. They wanted to know my nationality. This was a hard question to answer. What was I now? I did not know, and I did not know what they wanted to hear. Clearly, I was not a "real" German to these men of the Nazi bureaucracy. Was I a Pole then? No, not really, as I was born in Barsinghausen. I was a German, but they would not accept this as an answer. They also knew I was at least partially Jewish because of my father, though my mother was not born a Jew. I did not want them to write Jew on my papers, for obvious reasons.

My mother finally lost patience with their nonsense. "He has been officially requested by the employment office authorities!" she exclaimed. "He should get rations if you want him to work! Look at him. If he doesn't eat, he will die!"

My mother was a blessed person. Thanks to her, I was able not only to stay in Barsinghausen but also to receive regular food ration cards. They finally registered me as stateless, nondenominational, and half-Jewish and issued me the normal ration card for food that Germans got.

Unfortunately, I was denied my ration card for clothes. SH made sure of this. He insisted that I get no clothing cards. He would not let them issue me any even though I was badly in need of clothes. I had been wearing the same tattered garments for years. SH didn't care, and he seemed to take delight in being able to deny me.

Luckily, we worked in a garment factory, and my mother was able to sew me clothes to wear. She begged for money for the fabric and made them herself. I still had a suit from Poland, and I wore striped trousers from an old dress coat for work. This went on for about a year until finally, SH at the municipality office was drafted into the army. Only then was I able to get the clothing rations to buy the essentials that I needed without taxing my mother.

In 1942, our spirits were very low as we thought the course of the war was in Germany's favor; but my life was actually much better back in Barsinghausen. After having been in ghettos for so long, I felt I had arrived at the table of a never-ending banquet. Food was rationed, but it was enough to subsist on. It hardly felt like rationing at all. After life in the ghettos, the modest food rations we were allowed in Germany were a veritable feast.

These things help you understand the relativity of life. Suffering in the ghettos was so stark, severe, and all-pervasive. Compared to living in the ghettos, wartime Germany was just not so bad. When you have had it as badly as we did in the ghettos, you can be thankful for even squalid conditions. This was one of my personal lessons from the Holocaust, and it changed the way I viewed the world thereafter. Yes, my mother and I were living in small rooms tucked into the attic of a house that should have been ours. Yes, we were overworked and underpaid, much of our wages stolen from us. Yes, we were limited in rations. Still, we had family and friends who had it worse, which meant we knew we had it pretty good by comparison.

After about three months back in Germany, I was beginning to look and feel much better. I had put more weight back on and no longer looked like a sack of skin and bones. Life was so much better here for me. It was good to be with my mother again. It was good to not have to worry about where I would escape to next. It was good to feel mostly safe.

I was struck by the normalcy of life in Hanover and Barsinghausen. Despite the war being on all across Europe and the globe, the war seemed to have barely arrived there. Despite shortages and rationing, occasional bombings, and soldiers everywhere, there was also food on the table and music playing in the cafés of Hanover. Day-to-day life was more or less normal, which seemed amazing given that all of Europe was in turmoil.

Bombing Begins

This was in 1942, though, and things would soon change. Hanover was bombed frequently during the war because it was both on the road to Dresden and an industrial hub for the production of rubber and machinery. Factories and refineries vital to the German war effort made Hanover a key target for Allied bombers. The city had been spared these bombing raids in the middle of the war once France had fallen and England retreated from the mainland. By 1943, however, America had entered the conflict on the Western Front in force and the tide of the war had turned. Germany began to see increased bombing as the Allies launched strategic bombing campaigns across the land.

Barsinghausen was a small town and so was mostly spared from the heaviest bombings. Hanover, on the other hand, with its many factories and industrial centers, was not spared. It seemed that bombers came almost every night. There were approximately eighty-eight bombing raids in the city when all was said and done.

On the night of September 27, 1943, Allied bombers ran one of the deadliest bombing raids over the city. Some six hundred bombers dropped over two thousand tons of bombs on the city in the most destructive attack on the city of the entire war. Fourteen days later, the armada of planes returned and dropped another two thousand three hundred tons of bombs.

Hanover was in ruins. The official reports said that over six thousand people were killed in the bombings, but it was more like ten thousand. Another two hundred fifty thousand people were made homeless. The entire infrastructure of the city was destroyed. Few buildings remained in the city proper, including residential buildings. Over 90 percent of the city center was leveled by bombs, and many of the suburbs had been destroyed as well.

It was a complicated feeling to rejoice at my home country—my hometown even—being bombed by foreign powers. This was especially true with all the carnage the bombing wrought.

But rejoice I did. I was happy to hear that the Gestapo station was bombed not once, but twice. The more they bombed, the more I rejoiced. Each bomb was one more step toward the ultimate liberation of the Jewish people, Europe, and Germany itself. I had to remind myself that those bombs were necessary.

Germany and its people were not spared suffering during the war. It is easy to forget that many of the German people were also victims of Hitler's regime. There had been some opposition to Nazi rule in Germany, but it was silenced by the Gestapo. After the bombings, there was even more dissent among the Germans. The mood in Hanover and Barsinghausen was dour.

Official reports put out by the Nazi propaganda machine maintained that everything was going fine. They said that the Nazi regime was strong, and that the future of Germany remained bright, even as our cities burned around us. The official German position was that the Allies could not break the German spirit.

On the ground, however, it was clear that the German spirit was fragile. There was no official opposition; those who opposed openly were put to death, but the seeds of discontent could be seen and felt. It was just a hushed discontent. People were not allowed to complain, but they were frustrated by years of war, Nazi aggression, and senseless carnage and death. Now they watched as their homes burned around them and their loved ones were killed. People woke up and went to work to find that their workplaces had been bombed out. They returned home to find their houses burning. The world seemed to be coming to an end.

At this point, life in Hanover became much more difficult now that the war front had come to the interior of Germany. There was poverty and famine everywhere. There was disease. Many people in the air-raid shelters suffered and died. The city's economy had been destroyed, its infrastructure wiped out, and its citizens were suffering. People fled the city centers if they could to avoid the bombings. They fled to the countryside and hid in stables, in bunkers, in the woods—anywhere they could take cover and escape the bombings. This scene was playing out across much of Germany.

Barsinghausen did not take quite the beating that Hanover endured. The bombings were concentrated on the city, and we were a good twenty kilometers out from the factories and industrial parks of Hanover. Many residential areas of Hanover were bombed, sometimes accidentally and other times on purpose; but the Allied bombers mostly targeted the city centers, the railway station, the factories, and other strategic targets.

I saw my fair share of bombing raids though. The bombers usually came at night. Scouts would come in first, followed by the bombers. The planes would fly in very low and slow down as they approached. There would be hundreds of lights in the sky as the bombers approached, and they looked like a swarm of lightning bugs. Then you would hear a series of loud booms followed by explosions, and everything would catch fire. Then chaos in the streets.

When the bombers could be seen, you had to scramble for cover. You became accustomed to this precarious way of living, and it became the new normal—normal in the sense that it did not affect you at the time, but it did haunt you. I saw gruesome sights. I saw bombers shot down in midair. The German defenses would catch them in headlights and open fire with antiaircraft guns, and you could see planes go down. I always felt bad for the pilots. They would eject themselves, if they were lucky, before the low-flying planes slammed into the ground. I always hoped they would get out before the planes fell to the earth.

So many homes and buildings were destroyed—far more destruction than I ever hope to see again. But mostly it was not near us. Hanover was twenty miles away. From a distance, it looked like a light show at night. We never knew how close they would come though, so we were always scared. It was frightening.

In the days following the bombings, people would wander around homeless, unsure of what to do. It might be days before they received aid if they received any at all, and they were forced to find their own temporary shelter among the rubble. Some were sent to air-raid shelters, but as the number of refugees swelled, these shelters quickly became deathtraps for the hundreds of thousands living in them.

The other reason I rejoiced at the bombings was that all this confusion made our lives easier. With near nightly bombings, the Gestapo had a lot on their plates --swaths of the city were leveled, and hordes of Germans were homeless—their focus was not on one Jewish boy and his mother. The mass confusion and mayhem were to our advantage in this way.

As bad as it was in Hanover, Barsinghausen was spared the worst. Some of the bigger buildings in town were bombed, but not the residential areas. Our house had not been hit, so we still had a place to live and work from when there was still work available. Food and money became scarcer, and times were harder again, though it was still better than being in the ghetto. Life went on despite the carnage.

CHAPTER THIRTEEN

HIDING IN PLAIN SIGHT—AN INVISIBLE JEW IN NAZI GERMANY

M other and I had our own troubles in Germany. We toiled day and night at the Schmak company and for Mr. Brandt. Once I had recovered my health, I worked every day without fail, usually for twelve or more hours a day. This was more than acceptable though, considering the alternatives. This life was better than life in Poland and offered an opportunity for survival.

However, even this life was not to last.

After only a short time back in Barsinghausen, I was summoned by the Gestapo to appear at their Hanover office for questioning about my work papers (fig. 8A). My mother, concerned for my safety, accompanied me to the Gestapo station on Blumenauer Strasse in Hanover, just as she had accompanied me to the municipality building to apply for ration cards. I was still only sixteen years old.

Figure 8A

At the station, the Gestapo separated me from my mother, and I was taken into a room for interrogation. The officer leading the interrogation, a gruff man in SS garb, introduced himself as Officer Brauer. He asked questions about my background, where I was born, and who my father was. He was trying to figure out what my ethnicity was. My passport said "No Religion," but my new papers said "half-Jewish" and now I was to account for this discrepancy.

At one point in the interrogation, Brauer called for a special so-called Jewish "liaison officer" to be sent for and brought in. These officers were Jewish agents that liaised between the Gestapo and the Jews, mostly for the former's benefit. The liaison officer was Samuel Herskovits, a man that I had known from Barsinghausen as a child. He was a middle-aged Jewish man who had been director of the Jewish school in Hanover as well as the cantor who led prayer and the Jewish hymns we sang during worship. Herskovits confessed to Brauer that he knew me from Barsinghausen and his school in Hanover.

I do not blame Herskovits for betraying me to the Gestapo; he surely acted under duress. I learned later that his time as an agent for the Gestapo was limited. In the summer of 1943, he was transferred to a concentration camp and then in 1944 to Auschwitz, from where he never returned. He had betrayed me to Brauer, but he himself became a victim.

Brauer went into a mad rant when he found out that I had come back to Germany after having been deported to Poland. He demanded to know how I had been able to come back. I explained that I had been issued a work permit to work in the defense industry as a tailor, leaving out the parts about the deal my mother had brokered with Mr. Schmak.

Brauer still did not like my answer. He insisted that I had to leave again at once. "You do not belong here!"

Upon arrival, we had presented my papers to the Gestapo, including the work permit and letter of protection. I reminded Brauer of these documents.

"We shall see about this!" he barked. His plan was to have me deported again. He promised me that he would personally see to it that my papers were revoked and that I was sent back to the ghettos where I belonged. "This I will see to," he promised.

Fortunately for me, this was a promise Brauer would be unable to keep. Before he could see to my arrest and deportation, he was drafted into the military and sent to the Eastern Front, where, I later learned, he was shot and killed by the Soviets.

Even after hearing that Brauer was no longer at the Gestapo station, I still worried that my deportation would be pursued by one of the other SS officers. Brauer was gone, but he had likely given my file to someone else before he left for the war. All of the Gestapo in Hanover now knew of my case. Any one of them could have seen to having my papers revoked.

This probably would have come to pass were it not for a well-timed air raid on Hanover during which Allied bombers took out the Gestapo station on Blumenauer Strasse. The station was destroyed and many of the files were lost. This created enough chaos that the Gestapo dropped my case. They had far more to worry about than a sixteen-year-old Jewish garment worker.

Nevertheless, I continued to live in constant worry. The Gestapo station had been bombed out, but the SS simply moved their operations to temporary offices. They still operated in Hanover, and sooner or later, they would come for me as they came for all the Jews. I had to assume that I would one day be arrested and detained by the SS and shipped away to a camp somewhere. Every day I had to wonder, *Is today the day? Is this the day they will come for me?* It was not good to live under constant fear of death or enslavement day and night always asking myself, *Is this the day they will take me and work me to death? Is today the day they will murder me?*

The Dutchmen and Mrs. Liszy

Despite this anxiety, I went on with my life. There was nothing else I could do. I worked all day, and after work, I would spend time with my mother and visit friends. I made friends with some local Dutchmen in town who had also been sent there as forced laborers. These Dutchmen were prisoners of war who, like me, had been brought to Germany and forced into labor. This was how we met.

They had foreign worker visas, like me, and were also allowed to live freely in town rather than confined in a camp. This meant that we were free to travel around Barsinghausen and to Hanover. We often went into town to sit in the cafés and meet girls. For teenage boys and young men, this was the best part of not being in a camp: you could date girls. One of the Dutchmen, Theo Vandenberg, dated a Russian girl to whom he got engaged; but sadly, he died in an accident before they were married. Another of the Dutchmen, who we called Blond Willy, dated several German girls from around town, one after another.

They were fine boys and men, all of them, and were among my best friends in Germany. It was good for my soul to be surrounded by people you trust and who like you, after being victimized and betrayed so often. We lived like there was no tomorrow because that was very possible, so on the weekends, we had fun going into town together even when we weren't meeting girls. We would often stay out late and watch the bombers come through. When the bombs started to fall, the Dutchmen would whoop and holler with excitement. They hated the Nazis as much as I did. When the rumble of a large explosion sounded in the distance, they would shout, "Revenge for Rotterdam!" or "Revenge for the Jews!" and pound their fists in the air.

I also became friends with a woman by the name of Hedwig Liszy, who was even more of a radical than my Dutch friends (fig. 8B). She was an amazing and courageous woman who was born in Silesia, a contested area of Poland along the German border. Silesia was one of the first places invaded by the Nazis at the start of the war.

Figure 8B

I was enamored of and awed by Mrs. Liszy's life. She was a communist activist and a freedom fighter who had vocally opposed the National Socialist Party before they even came to complete and total power. She fought the Nazis on the Ruhr. She had spent two years in a concentration camp in Rünthe for striking a Nazi soldier in 1939. The soldier was prepared to fire shots into a group of communists with whom she was demonstrating, but Mrs. Liszy saw the soldier draw his revolver and took a swing at him.

Upon her release in August 1941, she moved to Barsinghausen with her husband and daughter. Though she appeared to have settled down with her family, this was far from the case. She remained active in the resistance movement against the Nazi regime. She and her husband worked in munitions and technical manufacturing.

Despite her role in munitions, she did everything that was in her power to cut the war short by sabotaging the manufacturing process when she could. She also spoke about the war to foreigners, especially correspondents, so that the world would know what was happening in Europe. When they could, their family provided relief to prisoners of war in Barsinghausen. She would buy large sacks of potatoes and distribute them to Russian POWs and the few remaining Jews in the Barsinghausen ghetto.

Her courage and perseverance made her an inspiration to me. I had my own struggles against the Nazis, of course, but they always seemed deeply personal, almost to the point of being apolitical. This woman had engrossed herself in the fight against the Nazis on strictly ideological grounds. She is to be commended for her efforts and morals. To this day, she represents to me the righteous face of humanity that is so prone to acts of tyranny. People like her, with her compassion and bravery, and selflessness, raise humanity above the level of vicious animals. If the Nazis, the SS, and the Gestapo were the dark side of man, the Mrs. Liszys of the world were the light.

I began spending a lot of time with Mrs. Liszy and her family. This was partly because I genuinely enjoyed her company and partly because she had a radio from which we could get foreign news about the war. My mother and I had no radio, and even if we had owned one, we would not have dared to listen to it with Mr. Brandt in the house. (I was still loath to think of it as *his* house.)

At Mrs. Liszy's house, we were free to listen to the radio as long as the volume was kept low enough that no passersby could hear it. We listened to Radio Moscow and BBC London almost daily. Doing so was not allowed under the Nazi regime, but many people, Germans and foreigners alike, did so anyway. The transmissions were often interrupted, and sometimes the signal was hard to hear due to the whirr of static from the Nazis trying to jam the signal. Despite the often-poor sound quality, we could usually tell what the broadcasters were saying well enough to follow the news of the war.

And that news was thrilling to us. On the radio, we were able to get news from the outside world, real news, not Nazi propaganda. Each day, we tuned into the news to learn of the newest advancements in the war. Mrs. Liszy had a big map of the globe that she would roll out onto the table we could follow the course of the war. We tracked where the war fronts were. We monitored how close the different camps, where our family and friends were held captive, were to being liberated by the Allies.

Taste of Defeat

We tracked the Allied forces that were beginning to pour into Germany. By the beginning of 1943, the fortunes of war had finally begun to shift, and the fronts were pushing not out from Germany, but back in, like an ocean wave that had broken against the shore and now pulled back. The Third Reich was beginning to crumble, and while it would be some time yet before the Allies would make their way to Berlin, the "thousand-year-long" Third Reich that Hitler had promised would be cut short by nearly a thousand years.

This downfall started with the capitulation of Friedrich Paulus at the Battle of Stalingrad—after a successful approach to the city as commander of the German Sixth Army, the Germans were forced to surrender.

Defeat in North Africa followed.

Then the Germans suffered a crushing blow at the Battle of Kursk. This was the climactic end to Operation Citadel, Hitler's plan to close off a bottleneck that would secure the Eastern Front. This was, and still is, the largest tank battle in the history of the world. There were also some two-million-foot soldiers involved. It was a major defeat for the Nazis. The Germans used thousands of Tiger and Panzer tanks, as well as several Elefant tank destroyers armed with a new 88 mm antitank cannon. The Soviet forces, led by General Zhukov, were outgunned. Their outdated T-34 tanks were not nearly as modern as the Germans'. Still, the Soviet forces held back the Germans and destroyed most of the German tanks. They then went on the offensive and attacked the decimated German forces.

This was the beginning of the German retreat on the Eastern Front. The Soviets may have been outgunned, but they fought valiantly and were driven by high morale and the desire to see Hitler toppled. The German Army was no match for whom victory was a matter of life and death. Many of the officers in the Red Army were Jewish. These so-called "inferior Jewish Bolshevists" proved themselves again and again on the battlefield, across the entire Eastern Front from Finland to the Black Sea as the Russians continued to advance westward.

Mrs. Liszy and the rest of us in Barsinghausen listened to the reports of these German defeats with glee. We rejoiced as we marked each defeat of the Axis powers on her map. When the Germans were ousted from Stalingrad, we marked it on the map. When Northern Africa fell, we marked it on the map. When the Allies landed in Italy and forced General Badoglio and the Kingdom of Italy to capitulate in September 1943, the first Axis power to do so, we marked it on the map and rejoiced.

The most exciting development though was the announcement of the Allied landings in Normandy on D-Day on June 6, 1944. While at work, rumors began circulating at the factory that the Allies had landed in France in a major land invasion. I couldn't wait for my shift to end. As soon as my shift was over, I rushed straight to Mrs. Liszy's house where the BBC was already playing over the radio. The landing was still in progress. There was little in the way of details at first from the BBC or from the German stations, but we did know that the Allies had landed, including the Americans, and that this was the beginning of a major push into the heart of Germany.

The importance of the entrance of American forces into the ground war in Europe cannot be overemphasized. Pursued by the British, the Australians, and the other Allies, the Germans began to fall back from Normandy toward Paris and then back into Germany. Now, we could begin marking the Western Front on our map as the Allies liberated France and began the long, slow march toward Berlin. The end of the war was now in sight.

Of course, D-Day marked another major shift in the war. The changes on the battlefield were obvious—the Allies were making slow but steady progress. It was a war of attrition once the Allies landed, and things went slowly at first. In the sixth week, the Allies finally broke through German lines and began moving faster across Europe. Mrs. Liszy and I continued to monitor events via the radio and mark up the map, now cluttered with drawn and erased frontlines drawn in pencil, and we hoped for the war to end.

The other big change brought about by D-Day was in the spirit of the German people. Most Germans no longer saw the war as winnable. They hoped for an armistice like the one that ended World War I. They wanted Hitler gone and for the country to concede. They knew the end of the war was near and that Hitler would lose. They were happy about it too. They knew Hitler was the problem, and it would be better for Germany to end all this madness.

Despite the change in sentiment, the German propaganda machine continued to pump out papers about battles that cast Germany in a favorable light; but if you read between the lines, you could tell that the Nazis were losing the war slowly but surely on all fronts. The German people were not duped by the propaganda because they no longer wished to believe in it.

Even Hitler's own inner circle was turning against him. In the summer of 1944, officers close to Hitler famously tried to assassinate him in a bunker with a bomb. The attempt failed—like the dozen or so such attempts that preceded it—but this one was especially tragic because it came so close! The bomb went off with Hitler in the room, but he was not killed.

For a brief time, it was reported that Hitler had been assassinated, but these reports turned out to be false. When the correspondents retracted their claims of Hitler's demise on the BBC, we were heartbroken. If only Hitler had died that day and the Nazi regime had fallen, so many lives could have been spared. But as it turned out, the war's end would not come for another eight months. Still, just knowing that even those in Hitler's inner circle wanted him dead buoyed our spirits.

Despite the change in German opinion of Hitler and the Nazis, it was still not safe to speak out against the Third Reich or to be disparaging about the war in front of neighbors. You still did not know who to trust. When people in town or at work talked about the war, I did not take part in the conversation or give an opinion. If I did not know them personally, I put on my poker face and said nothing.

Now that the end of the war was in sight, I was extra careful to stay under the radar and out of trouble. If we could just wait out the end of the war, my mother and I would survive. It was, after all, only a matter of time until all of Europe—Germany too—was liberated from the rule of Hitler.

Unfortunately, Hitler refused to relinquish his grip on power, nor would he abandon the Jewish genocide. Indeed, in those final years of the war, the genocide was expanded and hastened. It soon became apparent that I would not be able to wait out the war in Germany in anticipation of the Allies' arrival in Hanover.

With the Gestapo Once Again

In August 1944, only two months after D-Day, I was once more summoned by the Gestapo to their offices in Hanover, which was now at Hildesheimer Strasse. I went, as usual, accompanied by my mother. We were met there by an SS officer named Butterbrot. He explained that the files from the old Gestapo station had been transferred there, and the Gestapo had begun to rummage through them in order to find the last Jews still in the area. It was then that my incomplete files were found.

This Butterbrot had poked around in my files and seen that I was Jewish—not a converted Jew, like my mother, or a half-Jew, as my papers said, but a full-fledged Jew. Because of this, he said I would have to be sent to a concentration camp or, at the very least, be made to wear the Star of David armband around town, which I had not been doing and was not doing when called into the Gestapo headquarters. This was technically an infraction punishable by arrest and death. But Butterbrot seemed not that interested in arresting me.

The peculiar thing about this encounter was that Butterbrot sounded almost apologetic. He insisted that he had only just been transferred from the criminal police unit to the Gestapo and that none of this was his idea. He said he was only following orders. I told him I wanted to stay with my mother. Surprisingly, he said he would see what he could do.

Eventually, he let me go, but only after saying that if his boss, SS Officer Schmidt, knew about this, I would have been arrested on the spot and sent to the concentration camp in Mühlenberge. "If he was here, I would have to send you there now," Butterbrot informed me. He said that I would hear from them in a few months—it almost sounded like a warning.

This Butterbrot did not only have a curious name—his behavior was curious as well. Why had he let me go? Why had he given me his real name, as well as the real names of his boss and the concentration camp I was to be sent to? Why had he tipped me off that I was going to be arrested? In retrospect, it seems clear to me that he was trying to win my favor. He knew the war was drawing to a close and that the Allies were closing in on Germany. After the war, he expected that the Allies would hold the Nazis accountable for their crimes, especially the Gestapo. (Everyone expected this, though it would later end up being only partially true.) It was clear to me later that Butterbrot had called me in and made a big show of sparing me from his superiors because when the Allies came through and arrested the Gestapo, he would need people to testify on his behalf and prove that he wasn't such a bad person, that he was acting under duress, and that he should be spared. There was no other reason for him to call me in to *not* be deported.

I had escaped again, but this put real fear in me. It now seemed only a matter of time before I would be summoned for transfer to a concentration camp. In trying to save himself, this Butterbrot had given me fair warning of my impending deportation. If I were to escape when the summons finally came, I would have to plan now. I dug my sister's old bike out of storage and cleaned it up, taking all the rust off with an oily rag. I packed myself a travel bag so that I would be ready to go when they came for me.

I understood that if they came and arrested me at the house, there would be little I could do except to try to flee out the back. I hoped and prayed that when they did send for me, the summons would come by post, not in person from armed officers. This seemed plausible as that was how they had summoned me before, and perhaps this Butterbrot would see to it that I received a letter first so that I could escape and attest to his benevolence.

Five months passed before I heard from the Gestapo again. On February 8, 1945, a mere three months before the fall of Berlin and Germany's capitulation, I received a third and final summons in the mail from the SS office in Hanover. The letter informed me that I was being transferred from my official job assignment at the garment factory to a new assignment in the east. I was ordered to appear at the Gestapo station at Hildesheimer Strasse, which is now the Hanover Municipal Library, by February 19. I was told to bring a ten-day supply of food with me. If I did not come, they would come for me.

The summons was couched as a work transfer—but that was a euphemism. From Hanover, I would be transported to Terezín and then to Mühlenberge for my new work assignment. Thanks to Butterbrot, I knew exactly what waited for me at Mühlenberge—a concentration camp. No wonder I would need only a ten-day supply of food; they probably didn't plan to let me live any longer than that!

Finally, the day I had feared was upon me—I was being sent to a concentration camp. The Allies were already making slow but steady progress into Germany and closing in on Berlin. I had made it so far, and I too was now to be butchered, quickly while they still could. I had not survived all this time only to be slaughtered now. I resolved not to let them win. I showed my mother the letter and announced my plans to flee Barsinghausen. I knew that she would be in danger if I just left, and so we hatched a plan in which I would fake my own death. I wrote a suicide note and gave it to my mother to show to the Gestapo if they came to the house or the factory looking for me. The note claimed that I was terribly depressed and could not take it anymore. It professed that my transfer was the last straw. I wrote that I would rather be dead than have to go to the concentration camp, so I stated my intention to hang myself in the Deister. I handed the letter to my mother and instructed her to appear very sad when she gave it to the Gestapo. They would be suspicious, and it was important that she be able to deceive them fully.

I intended to leave that very night in case they came looking for me early. I did not know precisely where I would go, but I knew that I could not stay there. My mother and Mrs. Liszy helped me prepare for the trip. My mother packed me food and clothing for the trip, and Mrs. Liszy gave me ration cards so that I could stop and buy more food along the way.

Mrs. Liszy gave me the addresses of two people I could stay with for a few days while I figured out my next move. These were actually relatives of hers that lived in western Germany. They were sympathetic to the resistance, or at the very least sympathetic to her wishes. One of these people was a friend in Hamm, and the other was her brother in the neighboring town of Unna, Westphalia. I did not know how long I would be able to stay with these people or where I would go afterward. All I knew was that I could not remain where I was.

Before leaving, my mother begged me to please be careful. She feared that she had already lost one child—she did not want to bear the loss of two. "Be careful," she said. "Please be careful." She did not know when she would see me again—by this time, we had already confirmed the death of many in our family and so she was hesitant to let me out of her sight, but it was the only way.

CHAPTER FOURTEEN

PEDALING FOR FREEDOM— ESCAPING THE COUNTRY

A round five o'clock the next morning, on a Saturday, before the sun was even up and before Mr. Brandt had woken, I mounted my sister's bike and started on the road to Hamm. I rode the bike along the shoulder of the motorway, heading toward where I would stay with Mrs. Liszy's friend the first night. There was no way I could make it out of Germany in one night; it would take a week or so, which meant I would have to stop and find shelter frequently.

I pedaled as hard and fast as I could without running myself into the ground. Germany flew past me as I pedaled down the road. I passed many small towns along the way. First, Bad Nenndorf. Then I reached Porta Westfalica toward midday.

I traveled alone on the motorway for the most part, but I was especially worried about being stopped in any of the towns I passed through. I wasn't identifiable as Jewish—I just looked like a boy going on a bike ride. I was now nineteen, though, an age at which any young German man would have been drafted into the army. Not being in the army could only mean one of three things: either I was a foreigner, a Jew, or both. Luckily, I looked young for my age and could pass for under eighteen. I pulled my cap low to hide my face while I biked. I was trying to pass as a sixteen-year-old farmhand. I avoided lingering in towns where people would see me. When I stopped for breaks, I did so in rural areas and did not dally on the roads. I took my meals far enough from the roadway so that passersby would not see me.

Thankfully, no one stopped me in any of these towns. In fact, I saw very few people on the roads at all, perhaps because of all the bombers going overhead. On one rural stretch of road, I passed a chain gang of prisoners dressed in striped uniforms. They were supervised by armed guards. I didn't know who these prisoners were, but it was safe to presuppose many were Jews and Poles pushed into forced labor, as I had been. I kept my hat pulled low and cycled by them. Fortunately, I was not stopped—it would have been so easy for them to search me and find my papers, which I had brought along for use in Holland. It would have been so easy for them to put me in chains and hand me a shovel.

Near Porta Westfalica, I passed a platoon of soldiers digging trenches in anticipation of the Allied forces moving further into Germany. Again, I worried these soldiers would stop me, but they did not. The soldiers looked grim and low in spirit. I averted my eyes as I passed and continued along my way.

When I came to Hamm, I searched for the address I was given. It took me a while, but I eventually found it—a farmhouse on the edge of town. Mrs. Liszy had written me a letter to give to the homeowners, who were not there, so I gave it to the maid instead. The letter said that I was Mrs. Liszy's cousin and that I needed a bed for the weekend. The maid recognized Mrs. Liszy's address and handwriting and allowed me to stay in one of the rooms in the house. There were no difficulties there, which was a relief. I was very tired from biking all day, and my whole body felt sore. I wanted nothing more than a warm meal, a nice bed, and a bedroom door to close behind me.

I did not stay the weekend, only the night. The next morning, Sunday, I slept in late but then rose and packed my bag. I didn't feel comfortable burdening my hosts. After thanking them for the bed, I headed out on my bike and got on the road to Unna. Perhaps, I thought, a closer relative of Mrs. Liszy's would be more suitable for a longer stay.

The roads were again mostly empty. I passed bombed-out buildings and occasionally bombed-out houses. There were craters in the middle of the road from where Allied bombers had attacked German convoys. Allied planes passed overhead constantly, patrolling for more targets.

The planes were unnerving, but I remained calm and kept along my way. I was simply a boy on a bike, hardly worth wasting a perfectly good bomb on. I was no target at all as long as I stayed out of German hands; I would run the greatest risk of being bombed if I were picked up by the Nazis.

From Jew to Deserter

Later that day, I arrived in Unna and searched for the second address that Mrs. Liszy had given me. When I found the house, I knocked softly at the door and waited. This time, it was her brother that answered the door. I recognized him immediately due to the family resemblance. I explained that I was passing through town and that his sister had asked that he allow me to stay with him for a few days on her behalf. I handed him the letter she had given me. The letter claimed that I was a distant relative.

Her brother studied the letter and then welcomed me in, saying I could stay as long as I wanted. I met many members of Mrs. Liszy's family. Because they were all very nice to me and because I had nowhere to go after leaving their home, I did stay a short time. I got to know Mrs. Liszy's brother and his family and helped around the house. I couldn't stay forever, of course. Mrs. Liszy's brother was very nice to me, but I was not really family. I sometimes felt like a burden and as if I was endangering them by being there. My decision to stay for those few days was predicated on the simple fact that I had nowhere else to go.

Unfortunately, my host's son-in-law showed up at the house not long after my arrival there. He was a Nazi soldier who served in the Kriegsmarine, the German sea battalion. He was currently home on leave for a few weeks of vacation. This man took an insufferable curiosity in me. He started asking me all kinds of questions about my background. Where had I grown up? How did I know Mrs. Liszy? What brought me to the Ruhr area? So many prying questions!

"Why are you not in the army or in the marines?" he asked me again and again. "Why are you not serving your country?"

"I do defense work. I sew uniforms," I always answered.

"So why aren't you at home doing defense work?" he would counter.

"I am here to recover."

"That seems curious," he said leadingly, "what with the Allied planes bombing Unna every day and night. It's a curious place to come and 'recover.'"

He would not stop with these incessant questions! At first, I thought he suspected that I was a foreigner or a Jew, but soon it became clear that what he really suspected was that I was a deserter.

One day, he cornered me in the house while no one was around. "You know, in the marines, we shoot deserters all the time. All the time. These are fellow soldiers. Sometimes they are even our best friends."

I just stared at him, not saying a thing.

He continued, "Now, we don't want to, of course, but an order is an order! And our orders are to shoot deserters."

I excused myself and went to the room in which I was staying and lay down in the corner. My head was spinning with anxiety. I had nowhere else to go, but my current abode was becoming increasingly dangerous. This nasty brother-in-law might denounce me as a deserter. Being a deserter was almost as bad as being a Jew. If he called in the police, the Nazis would surely shoot me for one thing or the other.

I thought long and hard about what to do. Then I remembered something Blond Willy had told me. He was one of the Dutchmen I had made friends with in Barsinghausen. When I had told him how the Gestapo were harassing me and it was only a matter of time before they came for me, he advised me to flee. I said I had nowhere to flee to, so he wrote down his parents' address on a slip of paper and pressed it into my hands. They lived in a village not far from the border in Friesland.

Blond Willy had said, "When you go there, they will hide you."

This had, of course, crossed my mind before now, but I had not really entertained the idea. Getting into the Netherlands would mean passing over German borders, which was a risky proposition, to put it mildly. As a Jew and a forced laborer who was supposed to be in Barsinghausen, it would be difficult to get through the checkpoints without being arrested. I could be shot on the spot.

The Netherlands was now a warzone. The Allies had liberated half of the country earlier that year, which meant that there would be warfare, martial law, and much chaos. The border would be highly militarized. And even if I were able to make it over the border, I would still be in Nazi-occupied territory. The Allies had liberated parts of the Netherlands; but Friesland was still in German-occupied territory, which meant that there would be Nazi soldiers, Gestapo, and police everywhere. There was no guarantee I would be any safer there.

Headed for Holland

But what choice did I really have? If I stayed where I was, I would be shot as a deserter. If I tried to stay with strangers, it was likely I would be betrayed by the Nazis. At least in the Netherlands, I could try to find Blond Willy's parents and take refuge there. Even if I could not find them or if they were unable to offer me shelter, I would still not be any worse off than I was in Germany. If I could just make it over the border, I would have nothing to lose.

In the end, I decided to try to cross the border into the Netherlands, if only because I had to leave Mrs. Liszy's brother's house and had nowhere else to go. I was standing in the street, holding my sister's bike, looking very suspicious. Going to the Netherlands at least gave me something to do.

I hopped on my bike and rode toward Bentheim, which was the main German-Dutch border station. The ride would take many days. I traveled slowly now, without the fury with which I had pedaled to Hamm and Unna. I was in no hurry to get anywhere because I wasn't sure I had anywhere to go. Also, I had mixed feelings about trying to cross the border. I was still afraid I would be arrested or shot, a fear that only worsened the closer I got to the border.

I worked hard to buoy my own spirits. I reminded myself that I had nothing to lose and that I had to give this a try. I told myself that the Allies would eventually break through German lines and liberate the Netherlands. This was likely to happen long before Germany proper fell to the Allies.

Despite my efforts, I remained glum. I was lonely and desperate. Before, I had my family and friends pulling me and people to lean on for help. Out on my bike in the middle of nowhere, headed straight for the German border station, I had never felt more alone.

I was running low on food, but I still had some food cards, so I was able to stop along the way and eat at restaurants. I could stop for an hour, rest my legs, and just sit and eat. At night, I stayed in small inns that were occupied by soldiers, mostly older ones, who were also waiting for the end of the war. Often you could not get a room, certainly not a private one, because the inns were all so crowded. I slept in the same room with German soldiers. We stayed many to a room if we could get a room at all. Often, I slept in the haylofts of barns—anywhere I could rest my head safely.

Being around all these German soldiers was unnerving. Anticipating questioning, I had stories ready about why I was on the road. "I had missed my train." "I was wounded in a bombing and on my way home." As it would turn out, I never had to actually recite these fabricated stories. No one questioned me about my background or reason for being on the road. Many of the soldiers in these inns were themselves deserters. German morale had sunk low by 1945, and the Nazi soldiers were abandoning ranks and disassociating themselves from the National Socialists in anticipation of the Allies sweeping through the country and overthrowing the National Socialist government.

Many of these soldiers had clearly turned against their own regime. Often, we would listen to the radio in the evening. When regular programming was interrupted for announcements about impending nearby air raids, the soldiers would sometimes even cheer faintly.

Between air-raid-warning transmissions, the radio would emit clicks—*click, click, click*. One night, I heard a German soldier say, "Do you hear that? *Click, click, click*. Do you hear Goebbels running to the cellar with his clubfoot?"

Goebbels was Hitler's minister of propaganda, who had orchestrated Kristallnacht through the incitement of violence. Goebbels was known for having a shortened leg due to a botched childhood operation that forced him to wear a metal brace and shoe on one leg. The whole inn burst out into mocking laughter at this show of disrespect toward one of the most decorated of Hitler's henchmen. Even the Nazi soldiers now scorned the Third Reich and those at its helm.

After several days of crossing Germany by bike, I finally came to Bentheim. I stopped somebody to ask where the border was. One of the townspeople pointed me in the direction of the border station.

Before starting on my way to the station, I stopped to eat the last of the food my mother had packed for me. It was nothing much, just a little sausage and some cheese, but I was ravenous from so many days of biking and rationing my food carefully to avoid running out. Now, I had run out anyway. This last bit of sausage and cheese seemed like the last supper to me. It could really be my last meal.

After I finished eating, I stood and dusted myself off. I took one last look in my bag to make sure I didn't have any papers or documents at all. I had left these behind—what good would it do to have papers in Nazi Germany that denoted you as a Jew and a runaway POW? Once I was sure I had carried no such documents, I headed for the border station. I was quite apprehensive and second-guessing myself, but I resolved to see my plan through. Courage was all I had left in the world.

When I arrived at the station, I left my bike against a fence a hundred meters from the station and approached on foot. I approached the guard post where SS officers in black uniforms were checking papers. I could tell I had made a mistake by coming there. The man whom I asked for directions had clearly pointed me toward the most heavily guarded station. There were rank-and-file SS officers and SS officers who held the rank of Sturmbannführer (a high-ranking major). I approached the border post, my courage waning as I fought the urge to backtrack. I could tell from the stern faces that the SS officers did not take their jobs lightly. They had already seen me and turning around now would be suspicious enough to earn me a bullet in the back—there was nothing to do but approach the post as I had planned. My heart was in my throat, my stomach in my boots. It was all I could do to keep my facial expression neutral.

The SS officers waved me forward as I approached. Though scared and tense on the inside, I remained calm on the outside—my life depended on it. I knew that this might be the end for me, but I refused to give up without trying to cross the border. I prayed to God to carry me through, but if I were arrested, I resolved not to comply with their orders. I would not be complicit in my own elimination.

"Could you please show me the way to Holland?" I asked. "I'm on my way home. I want to go home."

They hardly even acknowledged what I had said. "Name?" one officer asked.

I gave my name as Theo Vandenberg. This was the name of my Dutch friend in Germany who had died in an accident. His name popped into my head, and so I decided that I would assume my deceased friend's identity. Perhaps he was watching me from above and dropped his name down onto my tongue.

"What is your destination?" the SS officer asked even though I had already declared my intention to go to Holland.

"To Tilburg," I said. Tilburg was already captured by the British. This I knew from listening to the BBC broadcasts on Mrs. Liszy's radio.

"Where are you coming from?"

"From Kunersdorf." This was a lie, of course. I had heard that Kunersdorf, now modern-day Kunowice and a part of Poland, on the eastern side of the Oder, had been conquered by the Russians.

The SS studied my face for a moment, and then without further ado, one of the SS officers drew a pistol and leveled it at me. He cocked the gun, a sound that I now fully understood.

"Hands up!" the officer said. "You are under arrest for suspicion of being a deserter. Step forward slowly."

The officer with the pistol walked around and behind me without lowering the pistol. "Theo Vandenberg, we are in the middle of a war. Military law prevails here. I want you to know that I can shoot you at any moment. One false move and you are dead. Is that clear?"

"Yes, Mr. Obersturmbannführer!" The officer was only a Sturmbannführer, but I deliberately exaggerated his rank to gain his favor.

This officer took me to the local prison by gunpoint, where I was locked away in a Nazi jail cell.

CHAPTER FIFTEEN

A DUTCHMAN IN A GERMAN PRISON—BECOMING THEO VANDENBERG

The prison was where they held people captured at the border. There were already a dozen other prisoners there, all locked in one cell.

The prisoners were of many different nationalities. Some were Germans, perhaps deserters, but there were also Dutchmen and Italians. I was fairly certain I was the only Jew, and I planned to keep this fact a secret. There was a reason there were no Jews here—they had certainly been shot rather than detained.

So, when my cellmates asked what my nationality was, I claimed that I too was Dutch. "I am Theo Vandenberg, Dutchman."

"You are Dutch?" they asked.

I nodded and said yes, that I too wanted only to go back to Holland like them and had been arrested trying to do so. I knew very little Dutch and did not even try to speak it—instead, I faked a Dutch accent.

"You are Dutch?" the Dutchmen said incredulously.

"Yes," I repeated.

"But you can't speak Dutch! You sound like a German."

"Don't talk to him," someone else said. "He's a spy. Listen to his accent!"

I faltered. It was one thing to pretend to be Dutch in front of the

Germans, but quite another to do so in front of the actual Dutch—of course, the SS officers hadn't bought my story either!

I stuck by my story. I claimed to have been in Germany so long that I had nearly forgotten my native language.

"Well, that is strange," they said suspiciously. They clearly did not believe my story, but they left it at that and did not bother me.

I took a seat in the corner and thought about my predicament. I was in a sorry state. I had to get out of there before the Germans figured out who I was or that I was Jewish. But how was I to escape a locked cell?

I began to ask the other prisoners if anyone else had escaped. To my surprise, they answered, "Yes, all the time."

They told me that someone managed to escape almost every night.

"How is this?" I asked.

They told me how every night they would call the guards and say they needed to use the latrines. The guards would then escort them to the latrines as a group. Once they were out of the cell, the prisoners would all make noise at once. Banging the walls and pipes and stalls, in the commotion, one or two of them would manage to slip away, jump the fences, and escape to Holland.

"At least one person gets away in this way a night," one of the Dutchmen said. "Very simple."

"Can we do this tonight?" I said. "I must get out of here."

"You'll have to wait your turn."

"But I have to go *tonight*."

"Why?"

"Because my case is different from yours!"

They laughed. "What makes you so special? We all want to go to Holland."

I grew silent. I had said too much. These new acquaintances could hardly be considered friends, and I could not trust everyone in the room. If they discovered I was a Jew and reported me to the Germans, it would be the end of me. I would probably not even be sent to a concentration camp—the SS would take me outside and shoot me on the spot and dump my body in a ditch somewhere.

Despite their suspicions and objections, several of my cellmates decided to help me flee that first night. We planned to do the same thing they had done the night before. After the sun went down, we asked to go to the latrines. At first, they simply ignored us. Then when the guards finally came, they brought a garbage bin with them. They unlocked the door and carried the garbage bin into the middle of the cell.

"Here is a bin for your needs," one of the guards said. "No one will escape tonight!"

They were already onto us, which should have been no surprise, if they really had been doing this every night.

Unbeknownst to me, my failure to escape would turn out to be a blessing in disguise. If I had been successful in escaping to Holland, I would not have had anywhere to go. The Dutch police would have picked me up, and when I could not show them papers, they would have given me back to the Germans. Success that night would almost certainly have meant my doom.

At the time, however, I was heartbroken. I was convinced it was all over. I slumped down onto the floor of the cell and went to sleep on the cold concrete. Resignation set in; there was no way out. I would die here, I told myself, and it was time to face that like a man.

From Deserter to Spy

In the morning, I awoke to loud knocking on the cell door. The knocks were in quick, rapid succession and very insistent—the Nazi style of knocking. Through the bars, a guard called me by name—or by assumed name. "Theo Vandenberg, come on out! You are wanted for questioning."

I was sure this was it—that I was now to be executed. Why else would they call me out of all people? I rose slowly and came to the door, ready to accept my fate.

Outside of my cell was the same SS officer from the previous day. "Come on, Vandenberg," he said. "I don't have all day!"

The SS officer let me out of the cell and locked the door back behind me again. He accompanied me back to the quarters. This time, he did not draw his pistol.

At the station, he took me to a locker where my things were being kept. Everything was still there—my clothes and other personal items.

In my pack were cans from Hanover wrapped in newspaper with different dates. I couldn't believe I had forgotten these! They gave away my story as a complete lie—clearly, I had come from Hanover, not from Kunersdorf as I had claimed. This was why they had called me out. How stupid of me not to remove these papers!

However, it soon became clear that the SS had not noticed the cans or at least not put two and two together yet. They sat me down in a chair and began interrogating me. "Who sent you?" they demanded to know. They accused me of being a deserter. Then they accused me of being a spy. But at least they didn't accuse me of being a Jew.

I started to protest yet again, but then I realized that being a spy was far preferable to being a Jew and that if I continued to protest and resist, they might start to wonder why I was on the run if I wasn't a deserter. So I gave my false confession: "Yes, I'm a spy and a deserter! I just want to go home to Tilburg in Holland."

"Why?"

"I am afraid of the Russians," I said. "I worked for Germany, and the Russians will surely send me to Siberia for this if they catch me here."

The SS gave a knowing smile. "I see now. What we have here is a cowardly Dutchman!"

I shrugged as if to agree. Better to be a cowardly Dutchman than a courageous Jew.

"Why don't you sign up for battle against the Russians?" the SS officer said.

"Because I am scared to go to war. I don't want to die."

"A cowardly, fearful Dutchman, indeed," he said.

The interrogation went on this way for hours with him pressing me and me acquiescing to his assumptions. When he called me cowardly, I did not protest; I nodded in agreement. He asked where my papers were, and I told him that I had lost them in an air raid.

Eventually, I was made to undress so that they could search me. I thought this would be the end of me when they saw my circumcision, but the same guardian angel that had protected me at the train station in Dresden must have blinded this SS officer just as it had blinded the German doctor. The officer made no comment about my circumcision. This should have been a dead giveaway that I was a Jew—or at least most likely a Jew, which was good enough for the Nazis. But he did not even comment on my circumcision. It was as if he had failed to notice—as if he had been blinded to the truth.

"Get dressed, Theo!" he snapped at me.

I quickly did as I was told, relieved that I was still alive and happy to be covered back up again.

"We must figure out what to do with you. If you are not going to fight, you at least must work. You want to go back to Holland? Fine, but you will work there."

"I will work doing whatever you want," I said. "I am a tailor. And I can do other things too."

The SS officer that interrogated me consulted his superiors. "What do we do with him now?" he asked. "We have a cowardly Dutchman here with no papers. He lost them during an air raid. He says he wants to go to Holland to work."

"Then reissue the papers," the superior officer said, dismissively. He clearly had more important matters to attend to and considered me a trivial waste of time.

The SS officer whom I had been speaking with took me to an office where he had his secretary make me new papers. He dictated the documents to the secretary. I listened intently as he told the secretary to issue me documents in the name of Theo Vandenberg. I watched as they wrote these up and stamped them so that they were official.

The SS officer then accompanied me to the local employment office and told the officials there to give me a preferred position. "This is a Dutchman, an Aryan almost like us," he said. "Give him a choice assignment and send him on his way."

And this is what the employment office did. They issued me papers and a work permit and assignment, all in the name of my dead friend.

I felt born again, with a whole new lease on life. No longer was I a Jew in Nazi Germany, not as far as the Third Reich knew. I was now legally Theo Vandenberg, Dutchman.

CHAPTER SIXTEEN

ESCAPE FROM A CONCENTRATION CAMP—MY LUCKY ENCOUNTER WITH THE DUTCH RESISTANCE

The employment office issued me a new position at a textile company in Nordhorn, which was a town along the border with Germany and the Netherlands. It was technically in the Netherlands but was now on the German side of the current border stations. As such, the town was still solidly under Nazi occupation even though much of the southern half of the Netherlands had already been liberated.

The textile company where I worked was called Neuhaus & Dueting and still exists today under a slightly different name. I worked there as a locksmith's assistant and lived in a Dutch concentration camp. I was the only Jew in the camp, though this was not known to anyone else, of course. The conditions in the camp were far better than what I had experienced at the Jewish ghettos in Poland and certainly better than the Jewish concentration camps. There was no barbed wire around the camp, and we could come and go as we pleased. It was more like quarters for workers than any kind of camp I had known.

Not everyone working at the textile factory had it so good though. The facility was predominately staffed by Russian women working as seamstresses—all of them forced laborers. These women, because they were Russian, were forced to live in a much worse camp nearby. The Russian camp was closed and completely surrounded by barbed wire fencing. Daily, the German guards escorted some three or four thousand Russian girls from the camp to the textile factory. In the morning, they were taken from the camp to the factory where they worked all day. At night, the guards escorted them back to the camp for lockup. To see these women abused in this way was very disheartening.

Though the Dutch camp was tolerable, I found myself rather lonely. No one in the camp trusted me because I didn't speak Dutch, only German. My papers that claimed I was Dutch didn't mean that much to the Dutchmen when I clearly couldn't speak the native language. Most of the Dutchmen believed I was a German spy and wanted nothing to do with me.

This was fine by me, as I was better off minding my own business. I worried that I would be discovered as a Jew. After all, who ever heard of a Dutchman that cannot speak any Dutch? If the Dutchmen in the camp alerted the wrong Germans to this fact, "Theo Vandenberg" might be discovered as a fraud. For this reason, I tried to keep to myself as much as possible. If people in the camp didn't trust me or thought I was a spy, I didn't force the matter.

I did make a few friends in the camp over time, though. I earned the trust of some of the Dutchmen. These men trusted me, even if they perhaps did not believe I was truly Dutch. They reminded me of my Dutch friends in Barsinghausen, and it was nice to have someone to talk to as I had no friends or family around. Still, I kept to myself much of the time and tried to go unnoticed to avoid attention from the Germans.

Bombed Out

I did not remain long at the textile factory. Within weeks of my arrival in Nordhorn, the factory was bombed in an air raid. The entire factory was bombed out, and the adjoining warehouse caught fire and burned to the ground.

For several days, we were held in the camp while the Germans decided what to do with us. I was uneasy, afraid that we would be sent to concentration camps, but this was not really warranted. The Germans treated the Dutch and the French from Western Europe far more humanely than the Poles and Russians from the east. As long as people believed me to be Dutch, I was safe. I did fear for the Russian women in the other camp though. I worried they would be transferred to a concentration camp in the east.

Morale was high in the camp. The Allied forces were pushing far into the Netherlands and France and closing in on Germany by this time. Things were beginning to move very fast in the war. Every day, people talked about the possibility of liberation. The camp buzzed with excitement.

Shortly after the air raid, the Allies broke through the German border, crossing over the Rhine in Wesel. Allied troops and tanks began pouring into Germany, and it was clear that it would not be long before large swaths of occupied territory in the Netherlands were liberated from the Nazis as the Germans pulled back to protect their fatherland.

In anticipation of an Allied invasion, the Germans came into the camp and told us that we were being relocated further into Germany. All foreign workers were being transferred to camps farther from the approaching fronts. They wanted to take us deep into Germany and put us to work in factories there.

The Germans that came to the camp were part of the *Volkssturm*, a paramilitary militia organized not by the German military but by the National Socialist Party in the final months of the war. The Volkssturm was made up of civilians who had not been drafted into the military yet and carried out the local defense and paramilitary operations in Germany. The very existence of such a ragtag paramilitary group was proof that the Third Reich was crumbling around us.

Slipping Away

The Volkssturm began rounding up the Dutchmen in the camp and preparing to march us to Germany. But I had no intention of going with them. Two older Dutchmen who had come to trust me were with me as all this was happening. I told them of my intention to go to Holland instead and asked if they wanted to come too. They took a moment to contemplate the proposal and then agreed to accompany me there.

The three of us slipped away from the group shortly before its departure for Germany. We retired to a courtyard from which we watched the Volkssturm march the other Dutchmen out of the camp toward Germany. The Germans did not spot us, but some of the Dutch did. They glanced back suspiciously over their shoulders. They looked fearful but resigned about being taken into Germany. They eyed us with suspicion, perhaps because many assumed I was a German spy, but they did not call back to us nor did they alert the Volkssturm to the fact that we had slipped away. We watched as they retreated slowly into the distance and then disappeared over the horizon.

Once the Volkssturm were gone, we were alone in the courtyard with no one to tell us what to do. We took a moment to observe our surroundings. The camp was empty, the factory a bombed-out shell, and the warehouse burned straight to the ground. It was a ghost town. The workers were gone. Even the Germans were gone. Finally, there was no one to stop me from traveling to Holland and leaving the country.

The two older Dutchmen and I promptly set out on the way to the nearby border. The border station was not far. We were technically already outside of Germany, but we had not passed through the station yet. We assumed that the border station would be abandoned now that the Volkssturm and the military had pulled back further into Germany. We hoped to face no resistance at the border, but even if we did, I now had Nazi-issued papers that stated that I was from the Netherlands. I presumed myself safe.

We were maybe two kilometers from the border station when we passed a Dutch farmer along the road. We greeted him. "Gute Dag," we said.

He slowed his approach but did not stop walking. At first, he said nothing. It was not until he was closer that he returned our greeting. He whispered to us in Dutch, "You are from the camp in Nordhorn? Listen to me carefully. Keep going straight on, right past me. Don't look back or to the side. There are still German border patrol posts. Did you not see them? They may be watching us through their rifle scopes."

This was entirely possible and likely, as we were only two kilometers from the border. We were probably in the range of sniper fire from the border station.

The Dutch farmer continued speaking as he walked by us, never turning to face us. He said, "Go into the town ahead. It is called Denekamp. It is a small town. There you will find a dairy farm. Go there and tell them your story, and they will help you. You will be very happy to see them, this I promise."

The man continued walking past us, not so much as glancing at us as he went by. We honored his request not to look back, and we continued on our way to the town.

Safe Haven

When we got to Denekamp, we asked around for the dairy farm, careful to ask only those who were Dutch and local; we did not want to be caught by the Germans if any were in town. Finally, we found a farmer willing to help us. My two companions approached him. "We are Dutchmen," they said. "We're coming from Germany, and we want to return to Rotterdam."

The farmer looked us over, sizing us up, and eventually decided he could trust us—likely because my companions were clearly Dutch and not German. I did not speak, as I did not want him to hear my German accent. He gave us directions to the dairy farm, which was a short distance away, and we headed there at once.

When we got to the dairy farm, my companions again introduced us as Dutchmen on our way to Rotterdam. They included me, denoting me as a Dutchman too. The proprietors of the dairy farm said to come with them, and they took us indoors to talk.

The dairy farm, it turned out, was the main headquarters of the local Dutch underground movement. We passed between two big milk kettles, through the back door, and inside a big hidden room in the back. This was a secret room hidden from the Germans. The room was full of members of the Dutch underground movement and *arbeitsverweigerers*. An arbeitsverweigerer was a Dutch patriot who refused to work for Germany—which I suppose is what I too had become, in a way.

The owner of the dairy farm was the commander of the local Dutch resistance. In public, he pretended to be a good friend of the Germans and even a Nazi collaborator. He often had German visitors upstairs, and Nazis sometimes frequented his establishment. But behind closed doors, he was a resistance fighter against Nazi occupation and a provider of relief to refugees.

I was amazed by the scope of the operation at the dairy farm. The local resistance had built a sophisticated operation complete with operatives, messengers, couriers, and even a medical team. There were nurses and doctors on-site at the dairy farm that cared for sick refugees.

They explained that they helped people escape Germany—the Dutch, Jews, Poles, and anyone else alike. They offered to help hide us with locals on various farms but informed us that we could not continue onto the border. "It is not safe. There are SS officers at the stations, and they are arresting and shooting people at the border. You cannot go on. You must stay here for now."

They told us that the Germans still occupied the IJssellinie line of trenches, an area that Holland had used throughout history to defend itself, most recently (and unsuccessfully) in 1940 when the Germans invaded. The Germans were now holding this line in anticipation of the Allied invasion.

"Everything is blocked, and you can't get through," one of the Dutch resistance operatives said. "Stay here. We have farmers who take in arbeitsverweigerer. We will find you a place to stay."

My two companions and I thought it best to listen to these men— they were, after all, in the business of resisting the Nazis and hiding people like us. The Dutch resistance gave us food to eat, and their doctors and nurses examined us to make sure we were in good health.

After getting our fill of food and checking out okay, we were ready to be taken to the hosts. The Dutch resistance placed refugees with various farmers in the area who were sympathetic to the cause. We followed some youngsters on bikes; couriers and liaisons for the Dutch resistance movement, they guided us through secret paths to our designated farmers. We traveled on back roads and through fields, avoiding the major roadways. They made sure we were not seen while traveling.

Most of the farmers could only hide one or two people at a time. For this reason, my companions and I were separated. My two friends were taken to a farmhouse where there was room for two, and I was to be taken to a different farm. We bade each other farewell and wished each other luck before splitting off onto different paths. I never saw them again, but I hope they made it out of Germany alive and well.

The other messenger, with whom I continued traveling, brought me to another farm and introduced me to a farmer by the name of Mr. Johansen.

"Ick ben Theo Vandenberg," I said, introducing myself to the farmer. I stuck out my hand, and we shook.

Mr. Johansen had a large family that helped him work the farm. They were Catholic. I pretended to be Protestant in order not to rouse suspicion for not knowing much about Christianity, hoping these Catholics knew even less about Protestantism than I did. Being part of the resistance, they may have taken in Jews, but I still did not want to divulge my religion—there was too much prejudice, and the risk for Jews was just too great. Perhaps this man only took in the Dutch and would turn me away if he knew I was a Jew through fear of being put to death.

The Johansens were very nice. I didn't speak much Dutch, and they didn't speak much German, but we both knew enough of the other's language to communicate crudely. They were a very poor family and struggled to make ends meet in these hardest times. Despite having so little, they were kind enough to share with me and others. Before me, they had taken in two Frenchmen who had escaped from prison in Germany. Because they had so little, there wasn't much to eat, but they shared what they did have. We ate milk soup with bread for almost every meal. It wasn't much, but it was enough. I had subsisted on far less before.

I stayed with this family for some time and helped out on the farm to earn my keep. I tried to stay out of sight during the day so as not to arouse suspicion. I did not want to get this kind of family into trouble. I often worried that someone would come looking for me, but many of the Germans had left the area and, while parts of the Netherlands were still occupied, the Germans did not maintain a presence in the rural areas.

The only thing keeping me going was the hope that the war would soon end. I wanted to be safe again and reconnect with my mother and discover the fate of all those I left behind in Poland.

CHAPTER SEVENTEEN

LIBERATION AT LAST ... BUT I AM MISTAKEN FOR A GERMAN COLLABORATOR

I n March 1945, the front lines moved closer to the town. We could hear the distant rattle and rumble of gunfire, mortars, and bombs. It was like a constant thunder in the distance. The front line was now only thirty or forty kilometers away, and we knew liberation was imminent. Once the Allies rolled through, we would be able to pass into Holland unharmed.

The Johansen family went into town to go to church regularly. One morning, Mr. Johansen's two daughters went into town for the church as they always did; but this time, they returned after being gone for less than an hour. They came running into the house, jumping up and down. They were so very excited!

The girls cried, "The Allies are here! We are free!"

I jumped up. "Where? Where?"

"They're already in town!" the girls squealed. They were ecstatic.

It was April 1, 1945. After five years of Nazi rule, they were finally free.

I too was beside myself. I jumped from my spot, flung the door open, and went racing across the fields. I ran toward the town, towards where the Allied troops would be. I wanted to thank them. I wanted to be free.

The Allies and Germans were still fighting. I could hear machine-gun fire in the distance, and I could see German troops retreating over a bridge across the river. The North Sea–Rhine Channel, which established the border between Denekamp and Nordhorn, flowed right by the farmhouse.

As I was heading up the road to town, I heard a very loud explosion and looked back toward the bridge to see dust, smoke, and flying debris. The bridge that spanned the channel had been bombed and crumbled into the river. The Germans had blown up the bridge to slow the advance of the Allied forces. Many German troops were caught on the wrong side of the bridge. They could not return to Germany now. Those left behind scurried around looking for hiding before the Allied troops found them. Some tried to cross the river on foot, wading across the water, and were dragged downstream. Trucks and buses full of German troops turned around, trying to find an alternate route. Such chaos is war!

The men of the underground movement came out of hiding and began hunting the Germans with the Allies. They captured and detained the German soldiers who had not been able to escape over the bridge. They probably had two hundred Nazi soldiers, SS officers, and other German officials in captivity.

For their part, the Germans couldn't wait to surrender. They had dropped their guns immediately and put up their hands. "Don't shoot, don't shoot!" they said. "We've been deceived by Hitler. We have been made to serve Hitler!"

As for myself, I avoided the soldiers and made my way into town. Everywhere the Dutch were rejoicing. Children and women wore sashes that were a bright orange—the traditional color of the Dutch royal family and a sign of Dutch pride. They hung the Dutch flag—with its blue, white, and red stripes—everywhere, tying it up with orange ribbon. Meanwhile, they took down Nazi flags from the municipal building in town.

I made my way to the town center. Surprisingly, there were few Allied troops there. There were only three military vehicles—a light tank and two armored troop carriers. This was all it had taken to liberate the town, though it was admittedly a small town of little strategic importance. The Allied forces were merely passing through on their way to other targets in Germany. Still, it was encouraging to see the Nazis fall back against such little resistance. The Allies truly had them on the run. Soon, the war really would be over.

There were about twenty soldiers in Canadian uniforms milling about in the town square. I approached them to ask where the army was. My English was far better than my Dutch as I had practiced the former in anticipation of immigrating to America.

"It will come," one of the soldiers said. "You have to wait."

I spent the rest of the morning hanging around the town square. I wanted to see the Allied forces roll through town. I didn't have to wait long. More tanks and infantry transports arrived later in the afternoon. Whole platoons arrived. The Dutch townspeople and resistance members cheered them on as they rode into town.

First, the Canadians came into town. They were followed later by the English. There was even a battalion of Polish soldiers—resistance fighters who had not collaborated with the Nazis. All these soldiers were greeted with glee and celebration, each of them celebrated as a gladiator, a patriot, or a liberator.

The Allied soldiers began to do systematic sweeps of the town and fields, looking for the last of the German soldiers. They went through people's houses and barns and yards looking for Germans. They caught few because most had already surrendered to the Allies. The Germans had been so ready to drop their weapons and surrender—it was safer now to be an Allied POW than to be a Nazi soldier.

In the town center, excitement grew as the Dutch cheered on the soldiers. There were approximately fifteen thousand residents in town, and almost everyone showed up to welcome the Allies. We waved to the troops and rejoiced and cried out, "Welcome! Welcome!" People began dancing in the streets and singing in groups. They sang the patriotic song: "*Het is oranje, het blijft oranje, het is oranje geboren, het leve die Koningin*" (a song about the monarchy).

Many members of the Dutch underground were present. They too wore orange ribbons. Many had brought their rifles to form an honor guard to welcome the Allied troops. Not all of us had guns, and so we used whatever things we had on hand in place of rifles—broomsticks, rakes, hoes, or whatever was at hand. I too joined the honor guard along with thousands of others. We cheered the troops as they went past. Everyone wanted to be a part of the parade. The honor guard's task was to keep the peace and ensure order. We kept the masses back so that the troops could pass through.

I was overcome with joy and a sense of unity. But then a curious thing happened: I was called out, not as a Jew, but as a *German*.

My Final Brush with Death

One of the young men in the crowd, who surely saw himself acting as a patriot, pointed at me and shouted, "That's a MOF!" This was a Dutch racial slur for Germans. Another of the men in the crowd, one of the Dutch resistance members, pulled a gun on me. He pressed the barrel into my chest and nearly shot me, just as the German SS officer had almost done in the ghetto when I was pulled off the street for a beating.

"Please, do not shoot!" I shouted, throwing my hands up in surrender. "Bring me to the commander! I am no collaborator! I am with the resistance!"

I was quickly surrounded. What an irony it would have been to have been shot then, not by the Nazis, but by the resistance—to be killed not for my Jewish heritage, but my German nationality.

They did not fire at me though. I told them I was no Nazi—that I was a Jew and that I could prove it.

"How?" they asked.

I proved it the best way I knew how: I spoke to them in Yiddish. "See? Please, take me to your commander. I know him."

They did not speak Yiddish, so for all they knew, I could have been faking it. But they did agree to take me to their commander. Of course, I already knew this person—it was the dairy farmer at the local resistance movement headquarters. He recognized me, as I had met him only weeks before.

"Theo!" he said.

This is when I divulged that my name was not Theo and that I was not Dutch. I told him my real name, my nationality, and my Jewish heritage.

"This man is no German spy," the dairy farmer said. "Let him go."

The Dutch resistance issued me a new set of identification papers in the name of Sigmund Weiss from Barsinghausen (fig. 9). They asked what nationality I would like to be listed as. I did not want to be listed as a German—not after this fiasco! It was only going to make people suspicious of me and get me into trouble again. The Allies had breached the German border and would soon topple the German government—it was a bad time to be German! Claiming myself as a German national could get me shot. Stateless was not good either, as I would have trouble crossing borders. So, I told them to denote me as a Pole.

Figure 9

"Polish it is," they said.

Thus, I was no longer Theo Vandenberg, Dutchman; I was now Sigmund Weiss, Pole.

The Dutch resistance then released me, and I was free to return home. I was still staying with the Johansen family. That night, we celebrated the liberation. This is when I told them that I was a Jew. "You have saved a Jew from certain death!" I said.

They were somewhat shocked, having had no idea that I was Jewish. This could have put them in great danger if they had been caught giving me safe harborage. They had undertaken a great and grave danger on my behalf without knowing it. Hiding a Dutchman in Nazi Germany was one thing—a Jew was completely different. There were only two other Jews in town, two young Jewish men. A farmer had only agreed to hide them because he had kept them in a cellar. They were only able to come out late at night when no one was around.

Once the shock wore off, the Johansen family professed that they were happy to have helped me and said they would surely do it again to protect another person in such need. They invited me to continue staying with them, which I did for some time while the war continued to rage on to the bloody end.

The next day, the Allied troops began to pull out of town. They were headed on their way elsewhere—to Emden, Bremen, and Hamburg. Eventually, they would make their way to Berlin for the final major battle of the war. It would be another two more months until the end of the war.

Free after Twelve Years

By May, only a few weeks later, news came over the BBC that Hitler had committed suicide and that Germany had capitulated (fig. 10). The war in Europe was over, and I was suddenly free. It was hard to believe, and the feeling was bittersweet. After six and a half years of war and another six years of rule under Adolf Hitler before that, I was finally in a free country again. I was nineteen years old now. I had been about six or seven when Hitler came to power and only twelve when the Jewish pogroms started. Hitler and war were all I had known.

Figure 10

But now I had made it out of Nazi Germany. I had survived the greatest nightmare of the twentieth century. I was free to go home to Germany.

Or to put it more accurately, I had to go home to Germany. In mid-May, only a week after Germany capitulated, the Dutch residents of Denekamp decided they would send all foreigners back to Germany. There were many Poles, Italians, Russians, and other foreigners—most of them refugees—in the Netherlands; and the country wanted them to return to Germany. As a Pole, according to my new identification documents, I was to be sent with the other Poles to a camp in Germany, near Lingen and just south of Emden. The camp housed former prisoners of the Polish resistance in Warsaw that had served under General Bor-Komorowski, a key figure in the Polish Underground State.

While I did not like the notion of being deported by force—it was too reminiscent of what the Nazis had done to us six years before—I did not resist arrest and deportation. I wanted to return to my mother in Barsinghausen. We had not been in touch since I had fled. I feared the worst—I had left her the suicide note for the Gestapo, but I had no way of knowing whether they had believed the note. I hoped very badly that she was still okay.

On May 22, 1945, I was deported from Holland and sent back to a camp in Germany. While the camp was not near Hanover, it was closer, and so I was glad to be taken there. The British transported us there. The camp was free, of course, nothing like the concentration camps under Nazi rule, but I still felt like something of a prisoner of war. There was a curfew, and we were not supposed to be out past eleven o'clock.

A few weeks after arriving, I was out late one night walking around the camp with a group of about six or seven English farm boys. We were stopped by British soldiers who arrested the whole lot of us and took us to a holding center in the jail for violating curfew. We spent the night in a cell.

The next morning, we were called in for questioning before a head officer—a British captain. He began questioning us. At first, he was angry with me; but once he realized that I spoke not only German, but also English, Polish, and a bit of Dutch, he took a keen interest in me.

"You speak English?"

"Yes, I speak English."

"How well?"

"Pretty well."

"How would you like to be my interpreter?" he asked.

I told him that I would be delighted to serve as an interpreter.

"Good. You can start immediately."

From Prisoner to Interpreter

I worked my first shift as an interpreter the next morning (fig. 11). I received no military training; in fact, no training at all. They found me a uniform of sorts, some ill-fitting trousers, and a shirt and had me come with them to a room where people were waiting in line to ask questions. Mostly it was prisoners of war that were trying to retrieve belongings stolen from them by the Germans.

Figure 11

I was sad to note that so few of the living prisoners were Jews—most of the Jews had been killed. Thus, it was to my great surprise when, one day, I heard people waiting in line to speak to the British officers talking to each other in Yiddish.

"Yiddish!" I exclaimed. "You are Jewish! How did you survive? I thought there was nobody left."

"No, there are some of us. There are lots in hiding, and there are more in the camps." They added, "Like yourself!"

This gave me hope and inspired me to search for Rosa. As a translator for the British, I was privy to many records. This was when I searched for Rosa and found her name listed at the Bergen-Belsen concentration camp, which was nearby. I was heartbroken. I ached to return home to my mother.

I received no monetary remuneration for my work as an interpreter, but I did get nice quarters in the camp. I had my own small private room. They treated me very well, and I enjoyed my job. It was rewarding work to work for the Allies, as I felt like I was giving back to those who had given so much.

But as much as I enjoyed my job as a translator, I still longed to return home to Barsinghausen and my mother. I could not return home though because there were no transports going there. Every day, I checked to see if any of the British transports were headed to Hanover or nearby, but they never were. I continued to work at the camp, waiting for a means of transport.

The camp was divided into two wings—one for women and one for men. Many of the people in the camps, especially the women's camp, were students from Warsaw that had been arrested during the war. One day, I was at the girl's camp visiting a female student I had befriended. While I was there, I saw an English transport truck. I asked the driver where it was headed.

"Bremen," he said.

Bremen was due east and halfway to Barsinghausen. It wasn't Hanover, but it was better than nothing. I asked if they would wait while I went back to the men's camp for my things.

The driver shook his head, saying he couldn't wait. If I wanted to ride with them to Bremen, I had to come along right away. There was no time to stop by the men's camp for my coat and money or any of my things. There was no time to say goodbye to any of the people I had met there. I dithered a moment before deciding to go immediately. I had already been waiting some time, and I did not know when the next transport would come or if it even would.

The transport dropped us at Bremen later that day. There we met up with occupying British forces. I was allowed to travel with a British military platoon from Bremen to Wunstorf, which is not far from Barsinghausen. I traveled there with the British and thanked them when they dropped me off. I had no money, no coat, nothing with me except for the clothes on my back; but I was mere hours from home. I set out for Barsinghausen immediately on foot. It was a three-hour walk.

Reunited with Mother

And so, on May 22, 1945, I arrived at my mother's house on Egestorfer Strasse, where she still rented a room from Mr. Brandt. I knocked on the door enthusiastically, and when my mother answered the door, she nearly fell over in shock.

"Sigmund! Thank God, you're alive!" she said. She looked as if she had seen a ghost, which was understandable given all the loved ones she had lost over the years. She threw her arms around me in an embrace, holding me tight.

I was glad that she was well. I would not have been able to live with myself if she had suffered because of how I had fled. She had not though. When the Gestapo came looking for me, she showed them the letter I had written. They believed the letter to be authentic because Mrs. Liszy and others had spread a rumor around town that I had hung myself in the Deister. This story appeared to be falsely substantiated when the body of a nun was found in the forest—the Nazis heard of a body being found and, without checking to be sure, assumed it was me. They harassed my mother no more after this.

All that was behind us now. She was safe. I was safe. We were together again. We had both survived the war, Hitler, and the Holocaust. It was all finally over, and the two of us, at least, were reunited. But the happiness was dulled by the knowledge that we had lost so many loved ones.

We lost so many people we knew. News of the concentration camps and death camps began to leak out across Europe now that the Allies were dismantling them. There were more camps than we even knew of—so many of them. There were at least three concentration camps in Hanover, which I found out only after the war while working as an interpreter. Thousands of Jews, many of them people I knew, had been worked to death in these camps. Many of them are buried in the Jewish cemetery in Hanover. More are in mass graves somewhere.

I heard so many terrible stories after the war. A twenty-year-old boy I knew from town had been sent to the concentration camp there and died in 1944. Others were sent to Auschwitz and Treblinka. I heard one story in which the elderly and the children of a nearby town were loaded onto boats to be deported in 1944, only to have the boats sunk by the Germans when the Russians blocked their route.

Up until the very end of the war, Hitler had plowed ahead with the

Final Solution. That was behind us—but I was soon to discover that the wounds and scars would endure for quite some time. Forever really.

Saddest of all, we had lost my father and my sister. We had learned the fate of my father and would soon have reason to suspect the demise of Rosa; but my mother would never truly give up hope that her daughter was still alive somewhere, somehow, and that she would one day return to us.

CHAPTER EIGHTEEN

THE FATE OF A FAMILY

I wish I could say that things had gone as well for my family in Poland as they had for my mother and me.

While my mother and I were working together at the garment factory in Barsinghausen, we were making money to send back to our family in Poland. Every few weeks we would send letters and care packages with money and supplies hidden inside. We wrote often, both to send money and supplies, but also just to stay in touch. Despite the escalation of the war, the letters almost always made it through to both my father and Rosa. Their replies also came back to us in Germany. They would thank us profusely and fill us in on what was going on in their lives.

In the subtext of these letters was increasing desperation and apprehension that made them hard to read. I did not care to think of my family suffering so in the ghettos while I was free to live in Germany. This was perhaps the beginning of my survivor's guilt—already set in before I had even lost my loved ones. But the letters from my sister and father stopped coming late in 1942.

It wasn't until after the war was over that I received confirmation that my father was one of the many Jews that perished in Poland in the terrible year of 1942, but I had suspected as much far earlier than that.

Not even six months from the time I fled Zakrzówek, the Nazis organized and executed a pogrom in the ghetto there. Nazi soldiers, SS officers, and Gestapo came into the ghetto and rounded up all the

Jews. Every Jew living in Zakrzówek was arrested and deported for extermination at various camps, mostly to Treblinka. Pinie and Rosa had already fled Zakrzówek by this time and were then, for the moment, safe in Pzyglow.

As for my father, he had stayed behind in Zakrzówek. When the pogrom started, he caught word of what was going on before the Nazis reached his apartment. He fled the building and the ghetto and went into hiding in the countryside. He met up with a Polish farmer by the name of Wassil Waremko who hid my father in the basement of his house. This man was a family friend we had met while living in the ghetto. I am still in contact with his daughter by correspondence to this very day, seventy years later. They were good people, and they tried to save my father from the Nazis.

Unfortunately, a neighbor or someone—we do not know exactly who—spotted my father at the farm and reported him to the Germans. The gendarmerie, the military police in Poland, came to the farm and threatened Wassil with his life if he did not hand over my father. He betrayed my father to the Germans, but I cannot blame him for doing so given the circumstances. He had no real choice. If he had refused, he too would have been arrested or murdered by the police, and they still would have taken my father as well.

The military police arrested my father and took him from the farm. He was locked up very briefly and most likely tortured until he revealed where his meager belongings were. My father had nothing but a few suits he had made and the other things that he traded for food. He had left these in two suitcases that he had entrusted to another Polish farmer. The military police escorted him to retrieve these trifles from this other farmer. The military police seized these things and then summarily executed my dear father in the field by gunshot. My father never saw the inside of a gas chamber, but he was a victim of the genocide just the same.

I have sometimes pondered whether it was worse for him to have died alone instead of part of a group as so many others perished. Who suffers more, the man executed in isolation or the one executed en masse in a gas chamber? These are ugly thoughts—but they were ugly realities then and therefore worth considering. The gas chamber is the more horrific way to go in our imaginations because it elicits terrifying images of the Jewish pogroms. It reminds us of the grand scale on which atrocities were committed. Individual executions happened frequently though—thousands of discrete deaths that add up to so much more. It is easy to imagine that dying alone is more lonely, desolate, and despairing than being put to death with your fellow brethren.

In both cases, I can only hope that death is some small comfort as an end to a tortured life. This is not to delight in death, of course. Jewish refugees did not take their own lives—they were murdered and horribly so. Still, I wish them all peace in death that they were not allowed in life. And I hope that my father, alone in body, did not feel alone in spirit when he left this earth.

As I have said, I did not know of this at the time, only that his correspondence had ceased; but of course, my mother and I feared the worst. She hung on to hope for as long as she could, as was her way. She never wanted to give up hope when it came to family. Eventually, however, confirmation came in the form of a letter, and any hope of seeing him again was dashed. We received a letter from one of the Polish farmers who had tried to hide my father. The letter outlined briefly what happened. The farmer said that he was sorry, but he thought we should know. I am glad he wrote to us in this way—it is better to know.

Reading the letter, I felt like I myself had been shot. I felt as if the bullet that killed Adolf Weiss had also entered me. I did not cry at the time. I was too shocked to cry. All I felt was pain, the palpable physical pain of my father's phantom bullet piercing me.

Still—it is better to know.

It is less clear what became of Rosa. She and Pinie fled Zakrzówek before the Nazis deported everyone from the ghetto. They traveled about three hundred kilometers west and settled in Pzyglow, near the town of Piotrków and, just south of Lodz. They stayed there for a short time, but by 1943, the Nazis were speeding up the implementation of the Final Solution. Jews from ghettos everywhere in Europe were being taken to extermination camps and disposed of precipitously. It was only a matter of time before Nazis came for them in Pzyglow as well.

The last letter we received from Rosa came to us in May 1943. Later that month, our letters started coming back stamped "RETURN TO

SENDER" and "ADDRESSEE UNKNOWN." We never heard from Rosa again. It wasn't until later that year when we received a letter from Pinie. My mother tore the letter open frantically, and we both read it. Pinie recounted what had happened to them.

One night in 1943, Nazi soldiers came into Pzyglow and rounded up all the Jews. They had received a letter that this was going to happen, that they were to be ready for transport. Normally, they would have fled, but this time, they were not able to get away in time. That was how it was in the ghetto: one day you would get a letter telling you that you had to report for transfer, and you had to go. If you did not go, they would come to your home and either kidnap or execute you. It was either go or flee—there was no stay. This time, Pinie and Rosa were not fast enough. For once, they were not ahead of the Nazis.

My sister and brother-in-law, along with the other Jews in Pzyglow, were sent by train to Treblinka. Upon arrival in Treblinka, the men and women were separated into different groups as was customary. This was when Pinie and Rosa too were separated. She went with the women and he with the men.

Treblinka was a death camp—not a concentration camp. The facility had one purpose: the efficient extermination of Jews and other peoples whom the Nazis considered undesirables. Almost everyone who arrived at Treblinka was executed within hours of arrival. The Nazis would deboard people from the train, order everyone to strip down naked and deposit their clothing and luggage in piles that would later be ransacked and lead their victims into gas chambers disguised as showers. They were then either buried in mass graves or incinerated.

While it was probably unclear to the murdered whether the gas chambers were truly showers or disguised gas chambers, for the most part, those killed were not unwitting victims. They knew that they would be killed, if not at that moment, then soon. It was said that the putrid smell of charred flesh and decay could be detected from over ten miles away. Most people probably knew their fate before they even exited the transport—they gagged on the smell of burning bodies. Photographs of Treblinka show massive stacks of bodies, discarded clothes, and suitcases. The Nazis' victims would have seen this detritus of human suffering upon deboarding the train. It would have been clear that the passage to Treblinka was a one-way trip for anyone getting off the transports.

Treblinka had few facilities. There were barracks where the guards and forced workers lived. The only other buildings were the gas chambers and the incinerator. There was no place to stay for people who were brought to Treblinka since they were typically executed promptly upon arrival. Only those few who were tasked with sorting out the clothing and valuables of the victims were kept alive for some time.

My brother-in-law was one of these men. They pulled him aside before leading people into the gas chambers. It was his job to search through suitcases and pockets to look for valuables. None of the Jews had much, but many had their few remaining little valuables that they would trade for food. The items weren't much individually, but they added up when you considered the thousands, the millions, of people who were "processed" at the death camps. This was a profitable income stream for the SS, who made Jewish forced laborers search for these valuables and hand them over before the belongings and bodies were incinerated.

Pinie spent long days rummaging through the pockets of the dead. He was also made to cart bodies from the gas chambers to the incinerator while German soldiers supervised. He saw so many people put into the gas chambers and then the incinerators. Thousands of Jews, Poles, political dissidents, and more—but mostly other Jews. Despite all the people that went into the gas chambers, Pinie insisted in his letter to us that Rosa had not. He said that she had fled from Treblinka when they arrived and managed to escape. He was sure of this, as he had never seen her body there. He had looked and had not seen her. The thought of Rosa was all that kept him alive.

His letter read, "My heart is like stone. I have seen so many of my friends and family go to their deaths and had to gather their clothes into sky-high piles. I can feel nothing more; only the hope of seeing Rosa again is keeping me alive. I cannot get over the murder of all my people otherwise."

Pinie had sent the letter not from Treblinka, but from a farm near Siedliszcze where he was hiding with a group of Poles connected to the Polish Underground. He had managed to escape Treblinka because he was young and strong. One night, he and two other Jewish forced laborers at the camp staged an escape. They left under cover of darkness but were spotted while making their escape. The other two men were both shot and killed, but Pinie managed to make it outside of the camp.

He fled into the countryside with his pockets weighted down with valuables he had taken from the pockets of the dead. He had stolen them in turn from the Nazis. With these valuables, he was able to bribe a Polish farmer into hiding him. It was from this man's house that he was able to write to us in Germany.

Pinie's plan was to wait out the war in hiding. The items he had made off with were quite valuable, jewelry and watches mostly, small expensive things that he could trade for a month of protection here, a month of hiding there. In this way, he planned to wait out the war in hiding until it was safe to search for Rosa. The belief that she still lived gave him the strength to push through. He loved my sister very much; this I know.

My mother and I were happy to hear that he was alive and had escaped Treblinka, and he had given us hope that Rosa was still alive even though we had not heard from her since they left Pzyglow. We hoped he would be able to find Rosa and flee Poland for good. We wrote back to Pinie at the address in Siedliszcze where his letter had come from. We never received a response. In fact, we never heard from him again.

Only after the war did we learn what happened. Pinie's younger brother, Schmuel, managed to survive the concentration camp he was in until the Allies liberated the camp. Schmuel made it through the concentration camp and today lives in the city of Afula in Israel. Pinie was not as fortunate as his brother, we learned from Schmuel after the war.

Pinie fell victim to a Polish gang. These gangs knew that the occasional Jew would escape the death camp and that when they fled, they usually took valuables with them. These gangs often looked for Jews in hiding to rob them of these things. One of the Polish men with whom Pinie took shelter betrayed him to one of these gangs. Though the gang let him live, they robbed him of everything he had.

They may as well have murdered him on the spot. Without his

valuables, he had no way to pay anyone to take him in. Without payment, the Poles wouldn't accept him—it was too risky. He had no family to stay with—they had all been taken. He had no one to turn to and nowhere to go.

He was soon picked up and arrested by the Nazis. In 1943, the Germans sent him back to Skierniewice. His only hope was that Rosa would be brought there too so that they could be reunited and escape together. This was not to happen. Shortly after being taken to Skierniewice, Pinie was shot and killed by the Nazi SS. I consider this act not only a personal tragedy but also a war crime. This was the end of a hero of the people of Israel. It was the end of an unarmed man murdered by his oppressors.

As for Rosa, what became of her is less certain. If Pinie was right, then she did not perish in Treblinka. There is some proof of this, though it is likely she was recaptured and shuffled to different concentration camps.

There are records that suggest she might have perished in the women's wing of the Bergen-Belsen concentration camp, a concentration camp in northern Germany, the same camp in which Anne Frank perished. According to documents from Arolsen, two women by the name of Rosa Weiss died in Bergen-Belsen shortly after liberation by the British, probably of typhus or exhaustion. One of these women was documented as Polish, the other German. Both were Jewish, of course.

Perhaps one of these women was my sister? Perhaps this was the same person documented twice—my sister? The recordkeeping was not great, and often the Nazis tried to destroy such documentation of their atrocities before the Allies came through and liberated the camps.

It is impossible to prove but probable that one or both of these records pertained to my sister. Presumably, Rosa was trying to come back to my mother in Germany, so it is likely that she would have given her birth name as Rosa Weiss and her nationality as German. Of course, Rosa Weiss is a fairly common Jewish name, and it is possible that neither of these women was my dear sister. She may have been sent to any number of concentration camps or death camps. She may well have been sent back to Treblinka if she had ever escaped from there at all. There is no way to know with 100 percent certainty. Seventy years have passed, and we still do not know, and now I am an old man and will never know. Up until the very day that my mother passed away, she still held on to some sliver of hope that her daughter would return.

Despite the uncertainties, I have decided to believe that it was my sister in Bergen-Belsen. If this is true, she is now at rest together with Anne Frank and many thousands of others in one of the mass graves at the camp.

Mourned and never forgotten by me and my family until the end of our days, until we draw our last breaths, together with all those dear to us: first and foremost, my father, my sister, my brother-in-law, my little cousin Shimon, two female cousins, two aunts, two uncles, and many friends and acquaintances who also perished at the hands of the Nazis. It is hard for me still to fathom the scope of it. The pain and suffering are at once so personal and so abstract.

Their spirits shall remain a part of me as long as I shall live.

As I have said, these tragedies revealed themselves to my mother and me slowly over the course of the final years of the war. It was not as immediate as I have presented here. Rather, it was a slow unraveling of the Weiss family. We learned a little here and a little there, and we held out hope of finding our loved ones, only to have those hopes dashed again and again. We had all been marked for death, but it was a slow march as one by one our friends and family were murdered.

CHAPTER NINETEEN

SURVIVOR GUILT—MY LIFE AFTER THE WAR

W hat I never could have guessed during all those years of suffering in Nazi Germany was that in some ways, the toughest part was yet to come. The atrocities were obviously immediately painful and difficult—but it was only after the end of the war that the quieter and subtler troubles began. This is the least heroic part of my story— between mid-1945 and February 1950.

I am hesitant to even attempt to describe the state of mind one finds oneself in after having spent years being brutalized daily, seeing your friends and family tortured and butchered. I hope that my story has already given you a taste of what I endured and a glimpse into my devastation. After the war, I felt like there was nothing left for me. I was in an emotional abyss that seemed to have no bottom. I tried to focus on the day-to-day, but the feelings of ennui and quiet desperation were almost too much to bear. Everything around me reminded me of all that I had lost.

I should note too, that just because the war had ended it did not mean that everything was alright for the Jews of Europe. To begin with, 90 percent of us were dead. The survivors had to carry the guilt of having survived. Those of us who had survived remained in rather abhorrent conditions even after the Nazis were removed from power. Many of us were still in camps. They were not Nazi camps, but the conditions were appalling all the same. The Allies had liberated us, but they did not have the means to care for us. Europe had been reduced to rubble, and many Jews found themselves in temporary refugee camps that became permanent camps because we had nowhere else to go. Our homes had been stolen and burned to the ground. Our families had been slaughtered. We continued to die by the tens of thousands in concentration camps that had been converted to refugee camps. We succumbed to malnutrition and disease just as we had under Nazi rule.

I suppose I was one of the lucky ones yet again. I had my mother, a place to live, and occasional work. I bounced between jobs. I worked as a machinist and a salesperson when there was work, and when there was not, I sold things on the black market for the money. I was just trying to earn some cash and put food on the table for myself, but that was hard, and it was even harder to find meaning in any of it.

I had no formal education, and those years seemed lost. I tried to resume my own education on my own by reading books, but this was of limited usefulness in terms of catching back up on my education. I was simply too far behind, and I feared—correctly—that I would never catch up again. I would never go to college.

I did the best I could to make a living in Germany. When I couldn't find proper work, I scraped by after the war in much the same way as I had in the ghettos—by trading and bartering. I worked in what would now be termed the black market. I hawked coffee and cigarettes and other such things on the streets. Many of the Jewish survivors did the same. Europe's economy was in shambles, and the Jews, having suffered such persecution, did not just bounce back immediately. In many places, such as in North Africa, Jews were still being persecuted—the Jewish pogroms did not end with the fall of the Third Reich. Anti-Semitism was still alive and well in the post-Hitler world, as it still is even today in some parts of the world.

Scraping by in the black market was all that some were capable of— and some were not even capable of that. Many survived the Holocaust only to commit suicide afterward. I was traumatized, but not as shell-shocked as some. Many Jewish survivors could not even communicate normally. Some could not remember what happened to them—their minds had blocked it out. They walked around dazed and confused, often physically and emotionally sick. It was hard to see so many of my people in this way. I began to realize that the Holocaust was not over—it had left a scar that would never heal, not for many, many generations.

Over the course of the next few years, I sank deeper and deeper into despair. I had lots of time on my hands but very little opportunity. I had no goals, and I struggled to find meaning in anything. I had no savings, no opportunity, no future. I began to realize that there was nothing left for me in Europe.

I wanted to go to the United States. I wanted to forget the past. I wanted to forget Europe. Everywhere around me, there were reminders of what had happened. I was aware that most of the perpetrators were getting away with what they had done without punishment. Maybe it was the easy way out, but I wanted to escape all that.

I had already made so many great escapes, uprooting myself time and time again-- what was one more? I had escaped from one ghetto to another ghetto. When they wanted to ship us to Warsaw and then to Treblinka, I escaped that also. And then I escaped Zakrzówek, thanks to my mother and the sewing machine and my job as a foreign worker— if I hadn't, I would have gone up in smoke. I escaped Barsinghausen by bike. I escaped death at the German border. I narrowly avoided being shot by many people over the years. One last escape to America, away from the ghosts of the past, did not seem so bad—it seemed like the only hope I had for a normal life. (fig. 12A)

Figure 12A

I told my mother I planned to leave Europe. I asked if she wanted to come too. I also wrote to my aunt and asked her the same. Neither of them wanted to leave—they said they were too old and that their whole lives were there in Germany. They did not want to start over again. As for me, I had had enough of Germany. There were reminders of the Nazis everywhere, and I wanted out.

It had taken me three years before I began trying to leave Europe in earnest, and it would be another two years before I was able to do so. It wasn't until February 1950 that I was finally able to board a ship to the United States. I had been accepted as a displaced person. I bade my aunt and mother goodbye and left Barsinghausen for a displaced person camp in Bremen, an important port and the site of a holding camp for displaced Jews.

After a few days, we were allowed to board a ship to America—the USS *General R. L. Howze*, a transport ship that was used by the US Navy in World War II. The ship was then repurposed to bring refugees to the States as a "liberty ship." If one was accepted as a refugee, there was no fare for passage across the Atlantic.

I had never been on a ship before. We were at sea for eleven days. There was a terrible storm along the way, and many people on board got terribly seasick. The boat was tossed about on the waves, but in the end, it was all okay. I slept in a small bunk bed in the hull with many other refugees. I too got violently ill, but I was free and very excited to see America.

There were many Jewish refugees on the boat, but also displaced Poles, Dutchmen, Russians, and people of other nationalities. What we shared was a desire to escape postwar Europe. There were even former Nazis on these ships—they were trying to escape their own terrible pasts.

We knew we had arrived in New York City when we passed the Statue of Liberty. I stood out on the deck of the ship with the rest of the refugees and looked up at the monument as we passed. Seeing the statue and what it represented had a great impact on me—just like in the movies. It really is breathtaking and awe-inspiring. We all had so much hope.

Life Stateside

I wish I could say that things were easy for me in the United States, but they were not. I rather liked New York City, though I did miss my family and friends in Barsinghausen. It was difficult those first months, but I received much assistance from the Jewish Center. They helped me connect with other refugees living in New York. The Jewish Center helped me build a social network and find temporary work.

I stayed with a friend from the Foreign Legion and his family for a while until I could afford my own place. I worked with him in New York, and we also went to Washington, DC, on a different work assignment. I got to see all the sites of America's capital city. It was a good time.

Upon arrival in the United States, I had briefly toyed with the idea of resuming my education, but I again concluded that it had been too disrupted by the Nazis. There was no catching up. Formal education in the United States was just as impossible as it was in Europe. My educational opportunities had been destroyed, and there was no real chance of recovering them.

Without proper education, my professional life in America was tumultuous. I struggled. I worked as a machinist and then worked as a salesman for a while, saving up my money little by little.

Once I had enough in savings, I launched my own business in 1957, along with a business partner. I started my own business doing the one thing I had learned how to do in Nazi Germany—trading. I launched a career as an importer/exporter of garments and textiles. I would import sweaters from Italy, export them to Chile, a dollar here, a dollar there, that sort of thing. It was all very touch and go, but I enjoyed the challenge. We made good money working in Chile, where they were sympathetic to the Jewish plight. (The country had taken in ten thousand Jewish refugees without requiring visas.)

I started new businesses every few years, it seemed I was always moving around, struggling to make money. In the 1960s, I went to Milano and started another business there. I started a business with my mother at one point, though it was short-lived. My mother had stayed in Germany and built a new house. I worked in Florence several times. I worked across the globe but eventually came back to New York City.

Not all these businesses did well; the truth is that my fortunes ebbed and flowed. Sometimes I earned a good living—other times not so much. As tumultuous as my career was, I was able to take solace in my family. In 1950, I had met my future wife in Café Éclair, a small New York coffee shop and eatery. This café was the site of regular social events for German-speaking refugees, which was how we met. We married on December 23, 1950, not all that long after I came to the United States (fig. 12B). Some people might consider this decision rash, but since we are still together sixty-five years later, I think it is safe to say that we made a sound choice!

Figure 12B

On January 31, 1953, my wife gave birth to Robert Weiss—our beautiful and brilliant son (fig. 13). Robert never ceases to make me proud and has gotten to do many of the things that I wish I had been able to do, such as attend university. In 1970, he was accepted into

Columbia University. We had little family income at the time due to my businesses struggling, but Robert, the brilliant and capable person that he is, managed to fund his own education. Between various merit awards and scholarships, he received what nearly amounted to a full ride to one of the most prestigious universities in the United States.

Figure 13

My son continues to make me very proud. I am grateful he has had the educational opportunities denied to me. He has since gone on to the Johns Hopkins University School of Medicine and risen to the top of his career as a dermatologist. He has authored papers and books and is a highly motivated leader in his field. I expect even more great things from him in the future. I could not ask for more in a son (figure 14, 1988).

Figure 14

I try to live my life now in a way that honors those who were not allowed to live. My family, the one I grew up with, was obliterated by the Holocaust. But I survived; and I hope that my own family, and my family's family, do well and live honorably and are kind to their fellow man. I have to believe that this somehow makes up for what was lost during the Holocaust.

These feelings probably amount to what is referred to as survivor's guilt. But I have found that by focusing on the future and not the past, and on what I have and not what I have lost, I have managed to make a new life for myself and find some happiness in this world. I have found there is no other way to move forward after you have lost so much.

As I have said, 90 percent of the Jews in Europe perished in the Holocaust, so many of my friends and family among them. Those of us who have survived best honor the dead by living as much and as well as we possibly can. I have seen a lot of tragedy in my life, but I have a good wife and a successful and honorable son, and I am comfortable. My father and sister and so many others in our family are gone, but now I have a son, grandchildren and even great-grandchildren; the Weiss family name lives on.

Here is what I have come to believe of survivor's guilt: it is ultimately illegitimate because the survivors had no say in the deaths of those who perished, nor did they have all that much to do in their own survival. I

Sigmund Weiss

resisted and I fled and did my best to stay out of the death camps—but ultimately, I was very lucky, time and time again. I owe my survival more to luck than to my own ingenuity or resourcefulness. I am not being modest—this is simply true.

My Hope for Humanity

No one person could have changed the course of history, but collectively, humanity could have altered the course of the Final Solution. If the Americans had entered the war sooner, maybe things would have been different. They could easily have stepped in earlier and bombed the railways and the crematoriums in Auschwitz, Treblinka, and elsewhere. They could have bombed factories and military bases. But they didn't. For Europe's part, it could have united earlier and stood up to Hitler before things got so out of control. And then there is the complicity of the German people. If the German military had laid down their weapons, if the people had said "enough is enough," maybe then things would have been different.

Because the whole world was complicit, the Holocaust happened. We cannot change that fact, but we can now say, "Never again."

I would like to think, "No, it will never happen again." But I am suspicious of the world's commitment to this statement, and the events of the last seventy years bear this out. I follow world events closely still, and time and time again, I am discouraged by what I see. I follow the Israel-Palestine conflict and the conflict between the Shiites and the Sunnis. At times—most times—these conflicts seem intractable. It seems like the cycle of violence always repeats. It is hard to watch.

In my more despondent moments, it seems to me that the whole world is crazy, the whole thing, and I have already had my fill of it. In the end, you can only worry about yourself and your family and those close to you—that is all that is within most people's reach. I want to support peace, of course. I want to do my part. But there is only so much any one person can do.

Other times, I recognize the power of collective action, and I am more hopeful. If my life experiences have taught me anything, it is that we must learn to love our neighbors, and if we can't do that, we must at least learn to respect our neighbors.

When I was a younger man, I tried to carry this message to the people. I have at times spoken publicly about my past, in Germany. Some of the German children were receptive, but many were blank-faced, and there was always a troublemaker or two in the crowd. Most of the children would listen, but there was always one skinhead or some neo-Nazi youth who would speak out against me and other "minorities."

What scared me most was not these lone voices of hate; what scared me most was the silence of the other children. The lesson of Nazi Germany is that the few can drive global change if the masses are silently complicit. The lesson of Hitler is that one evil man can change the world—if we allow him. It only takes a minority of fanatics to steer an apathetic majority. All it takes is the majority saying nothing, *doing* nothing, for the minority to commit evil acts. That is what happened in the Holocaust: a few people committed atrocities while many did nothing.

The Germans who were alive during the war have said that they would have done things differently if only they had known what was happening. They say they would have spoken out against Hitler, voted against him, dissented, disapproved, resisted—if only they had known.

While such claims of ignorance are spurious, there is some truth to this, perhaps. The Nazis were secretive, and it is possible that the worst horrors of the extermination camps were not fully realized. The German people did know about the ghettos, though, and many of the atrocities if not the full extent of what was taking place in the death camps.

In the end, it makes no difference: there were many who knew some of what was transpiring, a few that knew all of it—and both groups did nothing.

People claim they want world peace, but there will be no peace as long as there are instigators and a silent majority. There will always be instigators—it takes only a few bad apples to ensure this. That means that there will only be peace if the silent majority becomes and remains vigilant in speaking out against evil—only then can we truly say, "Never again." It is my hope that someday we will see that come to pass because

I wish only peace for my children, grandchildren, great-grandchildren, and their children and for the whole world, and I hope that nobody—least of all an entire group of people—should ever have to owe their survival to a virtually impossible combination of luck, courage, or miracles.